WALK THIS WAY

Hills, Thrills and Headaches on Scotland's Trails

GARY SUTHERLAND

BACKPAGE

First published in Great Britain in 2018.
This edition published 2018 by
BACKPAGE

www.backpagepress.co.uk
@BackPagePress

ISBN: 9781909430303
eBook ISBN: 9781909430310

A catalogue record for this book is available on request
from the British Library.

Typeset by BackPage
Cover design by Chris Hannah
Printed in Great Britain by MBM Print

MIX
Paper from
responsible sources
FSC® C117931

For Granny Stewart and Great Auntie Minnie,

the greatest double act I know

CONTENTS

INTRODUCTION

I am alone here in this forest, high above Loch Ness. A couple of miles back I was presented with two options: the high route or the low route. I chose the high route because it was my understanding that the extra effort would be rewarded with a superior view of Loch Ness.

But no. Having picked the more challenging path and endured the long climb, I arrive at a gap in the trees to look down on Loch Ness and am forced to admit that I can't see a flipping thing. Thick mist means I'm missing out; there's zero chance of me lording it over Nessie's swimming pool in these conditions.

My initial disappointment quickly gives way to mild panic. The combination of the sharp ascent and the realisation that the blanket of mist is actually below me produces the giddy sensation that I am high above the clouds and hence cut off from the world. It's an irrational feeling but then so is my fear of heights.

What the heck am I doing here? (You should have taken

the low route, YOU IDIOT. You'd be strolling along the loch shore right now... not stuck up here scared out of your wits!)

I am alone here in this forest, high above Loch Ness, and I am officially freaking out. In fact, I'm so far out of my comfort zone that I've ended up in the twilight zone.

I quicken my pace and race through eerie woodland – is there any other kind? – with nothing to keep me company except the fevered thoughts of a fast unravelling mind.

What if I take a wrong turn?

What if the path runs out? What then?

What if these misty conditions deteriorate to the point where I can't see my feet, never mind the path ahead?

What if I stumble at precisely the wrong moment and plunge head first into Loch Ness?

What if I'm being followed?

I look back.

Nothing.

What if a panther (yes, a panther) is stalking me?

I look back.

Nothing.

What if a Highland Yeti, like a Himalayan Yeti but ginger, is closing in on me with the sole intention of clawing me to bits?

I look back.

Nothing.

Phew.

I push on but soon come to an abrupt halt when my darting eyes pick out something unexpected on the path in front of me.

What *is* that?

It's a word. Spelt out in... pine cones? A few dozen of them carefully arranged to form a simple message in capital letters.

HELLO

Hello?

Clearly this message is intended for me.

By now, my paranoia knows no bounds. In my fragile state, this unexpected greeting makes me feel like greetin'. Or screaming.

Once I stop being frozen to the spot, I note how my previous quickened pace has been replaced by something akin to a sprint.

Alone here in this forest, high above Loch Ness, I find myself running for my life.

To hell with walking.

I HAD often seen them with their ten-storey backpacks, stumbling off the train and almost toppling over on the platform. The Walkers. With their heavy burdens and distant end goals, heading for the hills to embrace the back of beyond. Risking monstrous blisters and the midge menace for the seemingly sweet achievement of completing the West Highland Way. You'd never catch me doing that, I'd say to myself...

Not that I'm averse to physical exercise. A keen cyclist, I have biked the length of Scotland, while recently I took up running and completed my first half-marathon. But walking? I could never understand the appeal. I've long been suspicious of The Walkers. I mean, what on earth are they up to?

As an occasional golfer, I suppose I've done a fair amount of walking on the golf course but that's different. Someone once said golf is a good walk spoiled. However, I reckon they got it the wrong way round. Walking is basically golf minus the fun.

Besides the possibility of dying through sheer boredom, there were other reasons why I never pictured myself joining the ranks of The Walkers. For starters, I hate hills, my fear of heights being a big factor. Secondly, I'm terrified of wildlife (any kind, having once been chased by a cow). And thirdly, the thought of pulling on clumpy walking boots and having to wear actual 'outdoor clothing' appals me for aesthetic reasons. And therein lies the challenge.

Or so I said to myself one morning, while gazing out the living-room window at the distant Campsie Fells, when I got to thinking what an achievement it would be were I to somehow manage to do a long-distance walk. All those negatives which should dissuade me from even contemplating such a thing were now making me want to put myself through what is basically my worst nightmare.

Yes, living on the northern edges of Glasgow on the doorstep of Scotland's most-celebrated walking trail and regularly seeing The Walkers go wild for the West Highland Way had always made me think 'rather them than me'. But, and this may be down to my alarming arrival in middle age (my forties, for flip's sake), I was now thinking 'why *not* me?' Perhaps I could drag myself onto the West Highland Way and remain there until the finish line in Fort William. Maybe I would like to go a-wandering along the mountain track with my knapsack on my back.

While I have cycled round Scotland, I was pretty much seeing my country in a hurry, barely slowing down to take it all in. What was that saying about not hurrying and not worrying and being sure to smell the flowers along the way? Walking through Scotland might even be the best way of appreciating the place.

I may have always found The Walkers hard to fathom but I do recall bumping into a bunch of them once while on a long bike ride in Perthshire. I was struggling up a hill while they were skipping down it. Some of them may even have been whistling while they walked, they looked so bloody happy. Except all they got from me in exchange for their winning smiles was a dark grimace.

Yet now I was looking to join the ranks of The Walkers and see if I could begin to understand them. In the process, I might even learn something about myself too.

Being someone who has a tendency to bite off more than they can chew, I wasn't content to tackle just the West Highland Way. No way, Jose. I would also walk the Great Glen Way, which conveniently kicks off where the West Highland Way finishes in Fort William and concludes in Inverness. And that wouldn't be the end of the road either. No, siree.

Rather than being satisfied with a daring double, I found myself targeting an audacious hat-trick. Why not bag the Speyside Way too while I was at it? Upon completing the Great Glen Way in Inverness, I could hop on a train to Aviemore then traipse across Speyside to the Moray coast where I grew up.

Living in Glasgow for much of my adult life, one of the main things I missed from my childhood was being by the sea. The Moray Firth would therefore be a sight for sore eyes – and a balm for sore feet – provided I could pull off this trekking treble.

I had a quick look at the numbers. The West Highland Way was ninety-six miles, the Great Glen Way seventy five and the Speyside Way sixty six, making it a grand total of two-hundred-and-thirty-seven miles. Was that a lot? Was it way too much?

Not being much of a walker, I had no idea whether this plan of mine was mission impossible or not. Even just taking the West Highland Way in isolation, how much of a challenge was it? So I jumped on the internet and found a walking forum with first-hand accounts of the West Highland Way... and soon wished I hadn't.

One bloke said he was 'minus his two big toenails' by the time he reached Fort William. While the next post had me shielding my eyes from the computer screen: 'Saw a couple of lads in trainers and by the end of day two they had abandoned the Way with feet like a butcher's shop'. Note to self: don't wear trainers. Clicking on a different post, I was hit with another harrowing image: 'Feet like chopped liver'. Maybe this wasn't such a good idea after all.

But then there were those posts which made me feel less sick and more positive, the ones which were essentially practical advice delivered in a matter-of-fact manner and designed to ensure that the novice walker avoided a gruesome fate.

'Get good walking socks. Spend your money on them.'

'BREAK IN YOUR BOOTS.'

I vowed to heed those capital letters.

And I was further heartened by the words of those who had lived to tell the tale and who insisted that the West Highland Way was an experience not to be missed.

'It was worth it.'

'You won't regret it.'

Such sentiments made me want to set off straight away.

'Be ready for four seasons in one day,' warned one walker.

Hey, I'm Scottish. I'm used to it.

'Stick together,' suggested another trekker.

Um, it'll just be me by the looks of it.

After skipping the topic 'West Highland Way with

a baby?' I happened upon the following piece of advice: 'Don't carry what you won't need'. Like a baby, for example?

The truth is I was more likely to leave behind what I did need as my approach to packing can best be described as ruthless. I have a brutal sense of economy when it comes to filling a bag.

A fair number of people seemed to like camping along the West Highland Way but there was no question of me bringing a tent on my travels. In addition to being a reluctant walker, I am an incompetent camper. The only time I ever went camping was in America's Pacific Northwest during my year as an exchange student at the University of Washington in the Nineties. The camping trip, which was undertaken with my brother and two friends who were all visiting from Scotland, got off to a bad start with me leaving the tent behind at a Seattle bus stop. Somehow the tent was still there when I caught another bus back to the bus stop. But even with the tent in tow, the camping trip in the mountains was a total disaster.

The four of us, in our infinite wisdom, had brought along the combined food supplies of a loaf of bread, a packet of ham and a large bag of crisps, figuring there would be a shop at the campsite. There wasn't a shop at the campsite. We lasted one sleepless night under canvas in sub-zero temperatures, shivering and ravenous and hearing imaginary bears before I made an SOS call to Seattle the following morning (miraculously there was a payphone at the campsite) and pleaded with a friend to come and pick us up. So, no camping. What I required was a proper roof over my head and a comfy bed. Plus, the chance of a hot bath. Should there be tea-and-coffee-making facilities too, I would make good use of them.

While I wouldn't be lugging a tent across Scotland

– opting instead for a combination of hotels, B&Bs and hostels – I figured that I would be needing some other stuff on my epic expedition. I accepted, for instance, that I had to invest in a decent pair of walking boots. That and perhaps a pogo stick. I was actually half hoping that Scotland's Ways had been at least partly fitted with those travelators you find in airports. Or maybe I could just bring my bike? Two wheels good, two feet sore...

Nope, it was to be *à pied* all the way. At least there was zero chance of a puncture.

Blisters were a major worry, though. I didn't want to wind up with one so big that I'd end up giving it a name.

'Let's see how Barry's doing this morning.'

[Checks left foot]

'Ooh, wish I hadn't looked.'

Then there was the creature fear factor. My main concern wasn't even cows. It was panthers. The reason being that I once saw one lying in a field near Perth. I was a passenger in a car on the A90 at the time (no time for an eyewitness picture, alas) and now I couldn't rule out the possibility of me encountering said panther again, except face to face. What would I even do? You can't outrun a panther! Maybe I could give it a biscuit (I'd bring biscuits).

With all this weighing heavily on my mind as I geared up for my two-hundred-and-thirty-seven-mile solo hike through the wilds of Scotland, I drew up a list of potential threats:

Blisters
Midges
Mountains
Cows
Panthers

I then compiled a second list of useful items to protect me on my ultra-hazardous journey:

Foot cream
Insect repellent
Mountain repellent
Cow spray
Biscuits

Hills gave me the heebie-jeebies, moors made me tremble, blisters scared the bejesus out of me and panthers, although not indigenous to Scotland, were a genuine concern. To make matters worse, I also had a Devil's Staircase on my mind (it was part of the West Highland Way, apparently).

Nevertheless, I was intent on seeing through my hat-trick of iconic walks. A trio of traipses through the heart of my homeland and me not much of a walker to boot. Scotland. With sore feet.

As I prepared for this humongous hike into uncharted territory – for me at least – I kept telling myself to remain calm. What was the worst that could happen? I end up losing my shoes and my mind?

Nah, I'd be fine...

WEST
HIGHLAND
WAY

Nine o'clock on a Tuesday morning at the tail end of March and I stood bleary-eyed in Milngavie town centre next to a granite obelisk marking the start of the West Highland Way. While the locals were heading to the shops, I was venturing into the wild. But I was not alone. My friend Martin was here to give me a good send-off by walking the first dozen miles to Drymen with me before catching an afternoon bus back to Glasgow.

'All set then?' asked Martin, who looked every inch the walker, having done this sort of thing before.

'Think so,' I shrugged.

'Is that all you're bringing?'

It's fair to say I was travelling light. Nonetheless, I was confident I had everything I needed and nothing I didn't. Plus, I too had the look of a walker. For I stood in a pair of proper walking shoes that pleasingly looked more like trainers than boots. They were waterprooftastic Gore-Tex, just like my nifty new jacket. I was also sporting a pair of walking trousers, which to me seemed much like a pair of normal trousers in that they had pockets plus two lengthy compartments in which to store one's legs.

Keeping my toes snug were by far the most expensive pair of socks I'd ever purchased, as well as a second pair of not-so-woolly 'liner' socks (also not cheap). And, for the first time in my life, I found myself wearing a fleece jumper. While instead of a normal T-shirt I had on something called a base-layer top. I had John to thank for all this lot.

I'd had the good fortune to meet John two weeks previously when I had bitten the bullet and beaten a path to my nearest outdoor shop. He must have clocked me when I walked in, a non-Walker in a foreign land.

'Can I help you?' asked John.

I dived to the ground and gripped his ankles, pleading with him to sort me out and ensure that by the time I left his shop I would be fully equipped for a walk in the hills. Okay, I did nothing of the kind. I just muttered something along the lines of: 'Aye, I could probably do with a hand'.

I told John about my plans... well, two thirds of them anyway. I explained that I was intending to walk the West Highland Way and Great Glen Way but neglected to mention the Speyside Way for fear of sounding like a lunatic.

I mentioned that I was in reasonable shape but that I wasn't much of a Walker. John nodded and proceeded to bamboozle me with a bunch of complex walking talk – he could certainly talk the walk – but I concentrated hard and eventually tuned in to his frequency.

Although he lost me again, while measuring me for a pair of shoes, when he remarked that I had 'symmetrical feet'. As long as my symmetrical feet didn't fall off during my journey. I spent the best part of an hour with John and a surprising amount of that time was taken up by socks. Socks were important. If you had the right pair, in fact the right system of socks, then your feet would remain blister-free, simple as that. No need for any foot cream or plasters.

'Really?' I asked.

'Trust me,' smiled John, who was holding up a pair of socks with a £15 price tag on them. The thing was, I did trust him. John evidently knew what he was talking about. I thought about asking him if he fancied a pint after work, so that we could chat some more about this walking lark. But, ultimately, I decided against it because that would have been a bit strange.

So once he had kitted me out with everything that I needed, I bade farewell to my new friend and left the emporium of all things outdoorsy with John's words of encouragement ringing in my ears. My arms were laden with bags and my wallet was lighter but my confidence was sky high. Nothing was going to stop me now (to paraphrase the American band Starship).

Standing in Milngavie town centre two weeks later, dressed head-to-toe in John-approved walking gear, I wore over my shoulders a backpack that was barely bigger than my son's school bag. There would be no ten-storey burden for me.

The most important items in my compact backpack were a second pair of those pricey wool socks and another pair of the liner socks. Apart from socks, it also contained an additional base-layer top, a pair of non-walking trousers for wearing in the pub in the evening, a few T-shirts, underwear, a woolly hat, a pair of gloves, toiletries, maps for each of the Ways, a ham sandwich I'd made that morning, a banana and a water bottle. I also had a bundle of optimism – for the time being at least.

'Right, let's get going,' I announced.

'After you, sir,' replied Martin.

Perhaps he was mistaking me for Sir Edmund Hillary, in which case I could ask him to act as a Sherpa and carry my bag until lunchtime. Not wishing to risk ruining our friendship this early in proceedings, I resisted.

The two of us passed under an archway bearing the words 'West Highland Way' and walked down some steps.

I was on my way, so to speak.

Beneath a predominantly blue sky, we followed the waymarked path next to the Allander Water and were soon enjoying a morning stroll through Mugdock Wood. Our leisurely introduction to the West Highland Way continued as we ambled past Craigallian Loch before descending gently to cross the River Blane.

My new walking shoes – which I'd had the good sense to break in – were working a treat so far. Although I reckoned I might have been able to tackle these early miles in a pair of slippers.

Martin and I found ourselves following the path of an old railway line as we gazed up at Dumgoyne, the distinctive dome-shaped hill which stands at the western edge of the Campsie Fells. I can see Dumgoyne from my house and was pleasantly surprised to have drawn level with it midway through my first morning on the West Highland Way.

I was giving myself five days to reach Fort William. This required a daily distance of close to twenty miles. The average walking speed, I had learned, was three miles per hour. So I could expect to be on the move for approximately seven hours each day, which seemed doable rather than doolally.

Tackling the West Highland Way in five days is not at all uncommon, although spreading the ninety-six mile load over six days or a week is perhaps more typical. The only thing was that come the end of my five days, I wouldn't be able to put my feet up, what with the Great Glen Way and the Speyside Way also forming part of my ambitious itinerary.

'Ach, you'll manage,' said Martin, who himself had done the West Highland Way over five days, though he recalled that the Loch Lomond section in particular had proved a bit of a pain. I had the pleasure of that to look forward to tomorrow.

'What's so difficult about it?' I asked.

'There's just a lot of clambering around rocks and tree roots,' explained Martin. Clambering I could handle. Just as long as there was no climbing involved.

Scotland's first long-distance footpath, the West Highland Way opened in 1980 and remains the country's most popular walking trail, with around 80,000 people taking to it each year.

Several miles into my own journey I encountered my first fellow Wayer, who appeared to be struggling beneath the weight of his ten-storey backpack. As Martin and I caught up with him, the young man asked in an American accent: 'Are you a Huskies fan?' The question was directed at me since I was the one wearing an old University of Washington baseball cap with a big purple 'W' on it, the Huskies being the college football team. I confirmed that I was indeed a Huskies fan and our new companion introduced himself.

Sam lived in Virginia but was spending a year studying in Belgium as part of a university exchange programme. Since it was spring break, he thought he would make the most of it by coming to Scotland and walking the West Highland Way. Sam's love of the great outdoors, he explained, had been sparked in early childhood. Born in South Korea, his first memory was of going for a walk in the Korean countryside with his father.

'I would have been about four,' smiled Sam, who told us that his family home back in Virginia was just off America's famous Appalachian Trail. He was looking to reach Fort William by Sunday, which meant he was taking one day more than myself, but then he was carrying about ten times as much gear by the looks of it. Being someone who embraced the wilderness and who knew precisely what they were doing, Sam would be wild camping along the Way.

Martin and I walked with him for a bit, talking about life in general and Scottish weather specifically. The three of us eventually crossed a bridge over the River Endrick to reach the hamlet of Gartness, with its cute row of stone cottages.

Outside one was a small 'honesty' fridge, containing cans of soft drinks and bars of chocolate for the benefit of passing walkers. Helping myself to a Snickers and leaving my coins in the tin, I turned to find Sam propped up against a dyke, with his massive backpack at his feet. 'I think I'm going to rest here a while,' he smiled. Martin and I wished our American friend the best of luck and continued along a quiet country road for a couple of miles until we descended on Drymen, with its pretty village green.

On one corner stood the Clachan Inn – 'licensed 1734', according to a plaque by the door – and the two of us stepped inside for a well-deserved pint. I sank into a seat in the corner of the bar and took the weight off my feet. The cold beer tasted especially good after our morning's efforts.

With Martin the only other punter in the pub, I took the opportunity to remove my socks and put on fresh ones. This was on the advice of Martin's mountaineering pal Alan, who had recommended a change of socks every ten miles, insisting that it would make a world of difference. I was happy to take on board such a specific tip from an expert in the field. And I had to say... those few seconds in the pub in bare feet felt glorious. Martin didn't seem to mind too much. However, the barmaid may have given me a look. With my fresh socks on, I felt ready to take on the world. Or at least carry on as far as Loch Lomond before calling it quits for the night.

Meanwhile, Martin had risen from his chair and was

ordering more drinks at the bar. Sinking two pints in the middle of my first day's walking probably wasn't the smartest idea but then you had to stick to the rules. Two pals can't just go for the one pint in Scotland – you both have to get a round in.

After the follow-up beers, which went down just as easily as the first, we left the Clachan Inn, with Martin saying he'd see me out of the village. Except that after a couple of hundred yards we realised we were going the wrong way, which just goes to show how much havoc two pints can wreak on your personal sat nav.

Fortunately, we bumped into a bunch of Belgians, who happened to know the right way. The irony of two Scots having to rely on three Belgians for directions in our own country was not lost on us – even if we were doing a grand job of looking lost. The day also seemed to be developing a bit of a Belgian theme after our earlier encounter with Sam, the young American studying in Belgium.

Max, Louis and Matthias, *bona fide* Belgians from Brussels, informed us that we needed to turn back and that they were also walking the West Highland Way. 'Where are your bags?' I asked, a reasonable enough question given that all they appeared to have between them was one crumpled-looking map.

Max explained that their bags were being looked after by the two other Belgians in their party, who were having a lie down in a field nearby while Max and his crew tried to figure out what to do next. These Belgians, it turned out, weren't so much lost as stuck in a quandary.

Fully committed to wild camping along the West Highland Way, they had assumed they could pitch their tents wherever they pleased. However, they had just learned from some fellow walkers that local restrictions on wild camping meant they couldn't pitch a tent anywhere between Drymen and several miles up the eastern shore of Loch Lomond. Max, Louis and Matthias were wandering about the village seeking further clarification on this matter but neither Martin nor I knew anything about the wild camping restrictions. So we joined the Belgians as they popped into Drymen library to quiz the helpful librarian, who was able to point out on their crumpled map exactly where they could and could not camp.

Between March and October, wild camping was illegal between Drymen and Ptarmigan Lodge, with fines of up to £500 for anyone caught breaching a bylaw that had been introduced in an effort to crack down on anti-social behaviour in the Loch Lomond area, with unruly types leaving litter and general destruction in their wake.

The upshot of all this for our new Belgian friends was that if they were intent on wild camping this night then they had a choice to make. They could either walk another twelve miles until they were far enough up Loch Lomond for wild camping to be permissible, or they could stay put and pitch their tents on the outskirts of Drymen.

It had only just gone two o'clock. The Belgians didn't want to see their day grind to a halt this early but neither could they imagine trudging a further dozen miles with all their gear.

'We have more than one hundred pounds of luggage between us,' sighed Matthias.

'I could help carry some of it, if you want,' I piped up. This selfless suggestion somewhat surprised me as it really wasn't in my nature to be quite so helpful. Max, Louis and Matthias thanked me for my kind offer but politely declined. It was probably for the best.

'Are there any shortcuts to Loch Lomond from here?'

wondered Martin, thinking he could perhaps save the Belgians a few miles, thus giving them a better chance of reaching an acceptable loch-side camping spot by nightfall. The librarian nodded and pointed to the map. 'If you go up through the forest on the official footpath it's six miles to Loch Lomond,' she explained. 'Follow the road and it's three.'

Hence the Belgians would cut their journey time considerably if they temporarily left the Way and walked by the roadside for a bit. However, they were having none of it. 'But the scenery is the best part,' said an increasingly crestfallen Matthias. A shortcut was out of the question. They were resigned to calling it quits for the day before picking up the pace again tomorrow. It seemed a real shame. They had made such good progress on their first morning on the West Highland Way and now their momentum had been unexpectedly halted.

Martin and I commiserated with Max, Louis and Matthias, wishing them better fortune for the remainder of their Scottish adventure. Back on the village green there were more goodbyes, with me continuing on my way and Martin hanging about for the next bus back to Glasgow.

'Enjoy yourself,' he said.

'I'll do my best,' I replied as I finally prepared to strike out on my own. 'Thanks for joining me this morning... and cheers for the beers!'

I left Drymen on a country road, convinced I was on the right track until a man walking his dog informed me that I wasn't. He explained, though, that if I kept going in my current direction, took the next right and followed that road up the hill then turned left onto the forest path, that would be me back on the West Highland Way. He pointed across fields to trees in the distance and I thanked him

Walk This Way

for putting me right, while cursing myself for somehow managing to go the wrong way out of tiny Drymen twice. If I was getting this lost this early in my journey, how on earth was I going to make it to Fort William in one piece?

Then I remembered the maps in my bag. Yes, perhaps occasionally referring to a map of the West Highland Way while walking the West Highland Way would be a good idea. I dug out the relevant map to see where I was – and where I'd gone wrong – as it dawned on me that, technically, I had already failed. By straying from the waymarked path and re-joining it a mile or so later, I would never be able to say that I had walked the entire West Highland Way... Oh, what the heck. I decided that I was happy to play fast and loose with the rules. Were there even rules? Besides sticking to the actual path? Hey, it wasn't as if I'd taken a shortcut or hailed a taxi.

As I marched towards the forest in order to reconnect with the official route, I heard the thrum of a car engine behind me and was passed by a silver Jaguar towing a tree. Several minutes later, the same car came cruising back down the road, minus the tree. Maybe this was what they did for kicks around these parts? At least those with fancy wheels and an attachment to trees.

It wasn't long before I was entering Garadhban Forest and striding westwards towards Loch Lomond. I had successfully re-joined the West Highland Way – after a slight detour involving a couple of pints and some Belgians. Wandering along the woodland track and building up a heat, I stopped to remove my fleece. Too many layers. When I emerged from the trees onto open moorland a short while later, I was forced to put my fleece back on due to the stiff, cold breeze.

Turning my gaze south, I noted Dumgoyne in the

distance. It looked miles away, which it was. A definite sign of progress. The more relevant hill now, though, was the one ahead of me. Conic Hill was about all that stood between me and the loch-side village of Balmaha, my destination for this first night on the West Highland Way.

I crossed a burn and clambered over a stile and although I was gaining ground on Conic Hill, it never seemed to get any nearer. If anything, it appeared to be moving further away from me. Perhaps it was some sort of optical illusion, or maybe it was simply the fact that I was tiring. My legs were heavy and I was feeling twinges of pain in my left shoulder. Certainly my pace had dropped, those two beers back in Drymen having no doubt affected my three-miles-an-hour average.

The sky had clouded over and was threatening rain. Fixing my eyes on the ground, I tried to forget about the remaining distance and solely focus on each step. When I next looked up, it was as if Conic Hill had snuck up on me and so I began a gradual climb on the stony path that snaked round the north side of the hill. Once I had gained some height, I stopped for a second and heard it. The silence. It was as if someone had pressed the mute button – even the wind had gone quiet – and I tried to remember the last time I'd experienced such an absence of sound.

The silence was only broken by the crunch of my shoes on the ground as I resumed my steady progress. I noticed another path branching off to my left, leading to the summit of Conic Hill and I could see two figures up there. While it looked like the shortest of walks to the top, I dismissed the opportunity. Not so much due to tiredness but because of my difficulty with heights and the fact that it was beginning to get quite blustery again.

Having turned down the chance to go higher, I rounded

a corner and issued a loud expletive. This was followed by my own stunned silence. Before me – below me even – lay Loch Lomond in all its glory. Standing over this dramatic expanse of dark water dotted with tiny islands, I felt as if I could dive straight in. I also felt quite dizzy… it was high time I got off this hill. I made heavy weather of the descent, stumbling down some awkward stone steps.

At one point, I heard something behind me, the sound of rapid movement – an animal, perhaps? I swung round to see a wiry figure springing towards me. A hill runner, skipping from stone to stone like a human mountain goat. I stood aside to let him pass and watched him swiftly disappear from view. To think that folk indulged in such activities… I was only just getting my head round walking.

When I reached the bottom of Conic Hill, I followed the path through some trees and arrived at a large car park. Not the most glamorous of finishes to my first day on the West Highland Way but at the far end of the car park was my hotel for the night. I had bagged a spring bargain on a single room at the Oak Tree Inn and after checking in I staggered upstairs, threw my bag on the bed and made myself a coffee before having a long hot bath.

After donning my evening wear of fresh T-shirt and non-walking trousers, I wandered down to the bar where I enjoyed a plate of 'locally caught' haggis and a pint of Loch Lomond ale in front of the roaring log fire. With my belly full and the heat from the flames making me drowsy, I stumbled back up to my cosy room where, not surprisingly, sleep came easily.

— Day Two
West Highland Way
Balmaha to Inverarnan
Twenty-two miles

Mercifully free of aches and pains after the deepest of sleeps and determined to make an early start, I was the first guest down to breakfast in the hotel dining room. The waitress took my order of a full Scottish and asked if I would like tea or coffee.

'Coffee, please,' I replied.

'Right you are,' she said, wandering off only to return a moment later. 'Sorry, what was it you wanted to drink again?'

'Um...'

I'd quite forgotten too but then I remembered. 'Coffee.'

'I've got it this time... it's too early in the day for me,' laughed the waitress by way of explaining her forgetfulness.

'It's too early for me too,' I smiled through my morning haze. The coffee duly arrived and was swiftly followed by my full Scottish breakfast, featuring the surprise bonus item of haggis. ('This'll set me up for the day,' I thought. There was every chance it would fire me to the top end of Loch Lomond.)

Having cleaned my plate and checked out at reception, I popped to the handy shop next door and picked up some supplies, selecting a tuna roll, a packet of oatcakes, a Mars bar and a banana to sustain me over the coming hours. Although having just tackled the breakfast of champions, I couldn't see me facing that tuna roll until a week Friday.

Backpack slung over my shoulders again, I was on the march by eight, the low-lying sun shining in a pale blue sky and a thin layer of mist hanging over the loch. I passed some ducks by the shoreline and one of them decided to join me, as if they fancied being my companion for the day. I came to a halt and gave it a look. The duck got the message, did a swift about-turn and waddled off back to its mates.

No sooner had I begun walking again when I felt a sharp pain in my left heel, sore enough to make me wince. To be hobbling at this stage was a cause for concern but thankfully the pain wore off after a few minutes as I faced an early climb through the trees.

Such was my vantage point from the top of the wooded slope that I could see right up and down Loch Lomond. What a treat for my bleary eyes... who wouldn't want to be up first thing to experience this? I was a night owl who had just discovered that they were a morning person.

Loch Lomond is Scotland's third longest loch (after Loch Awe and Loch Ness). It is twenty-four miles in length, with the West Highland Way hugging its eastern shore for most of those miles. It was safe to say that Loch Lomond would be with me for much of the day.

I wondered what the chances were of me not seeing another soul during my walk to the north end of the loch. March wasn't exactly peak season for the West Highland Way, although John in the outdoor shop had approved of my timing for a couple of reasons. There would be no shortage of accommodation and, more importantly, no midges, with the Scottish insect menace specialising in making life a misery for walkers during the summer months.

But I had wondered how quiet the route might be. Prior to setting off, the prospect of extended periods of isolation had concerned me more than the actual distance, the unpredictable weather or any other aspect of my trek across Scotland. My boldest decision had been to commit to doing this journey alone (save for those first twelve miles with my friend Martin). But having stood on Conic Hill last night, savouring the silence, and to now be blessed with the morning glory of my own wide window on Loch Lomond, I was almost hoping I could walk for the rest of the day without bumping into anyone.

I left my high perch and zigzagged down through the trees to join a shoreline path for a bit. Caught up in the simple rhythm of walking, I sank into a daydream but was awakened from my reverie when my watch beeped to signal that it was nine o'clock.

Normally I never wore a watch but I had bought a cheap Casio number specifically for the trip as a back-up to the alarm on my phone. However, the blasted thing had been going off at hourly intervals ever since I went to bed last night. Somehow I had managed to set the alarm on my budget timepiece so that it went off every hour. Thus I had been woken at sixty-minute intervals throughout the night but had been far too knackered to reach out to the offending device on the bedside table and do anything about these frequent interruptions to my sleep. No wonder I still felt tired…

Pausing on a stone bridge to gaze down at the stream flowing beneath it, my legs seized up. It was probably best to keep walking...

Before I did, I quickly checked my phone and saw that I'd received a text from my wife. She and the children had been watching The NeverEnding Story in my absence and my daughter was thinking that Daddy's journey could be made more exciting by him pretending to be on an epic quest like Atreyu, the boy warrior in the Eighties fantasy movie.

I replied that Daddy's journey would certainly be a whole lot easier if a Luck Dragon – such as the one in the film – was to swoop down and fly him to Fort William.

With no Luck Dragon seemingly available in the Loch Lomond area, I was forced to rely on my own abilities and put in some extra graft as the Way rose over a ridge for another climb through woodland. The slightest incline seemed to require an immense amount of effort and I wasn't sure whether this was due to the earliness of the day, my lack of sleep because of that bleeping watch, the weight of my bag (which wasn't much, to be fair), the effect of yesterday's exertions on my legs, or a combination of all of these factors.

At least the trees had thinned out to afford me another gobsmacking view of Loch Lomond from a lofty position. I stopped for a top-up of joy and was further cheered by the fact that my legs didn't seize up. Long-distance walking, I had discovered already, was a physical and emotional rollercoaster, full of ups and downs.

With my fleece crammed back in my bag and my jacket tied around my waist, I was down to just the base-layer top, what with all this energy being expended and the sun beating down on me. It was a Scotland-in-early-springtime sun, not exactly Ibiza at the height of summer, but still enough to make me wilt.

As I plodded along among the trees, my mind drifted to The NeverEnding Story, a movie I'd watched at least a dozen times on VHS when I was a kid. Specifically, I was picturing the warrior-hero Atreyu trudging through exactly this sort of forested landscape, trying to fulfil his quest of preventing a malevolent storm known as The Nothing from destroying the fair land of Fantasia. However, Atreyu is unaware that he is being hunted down by a terrifying beast whose name I couldn't quite recall, but who was basically a cross between a panther and a really scary Alsatian.

Whilst replaying this traumatic scene in my head (hey, I'd no one to talk to) I heard a strange clicking sound close by. Then I imagined it to be a grunt. I had read that there were feral goats around the eastern shore of Loch Lomond. Could it be the goats, or worse still a panther? Or worse than that the half-panther, half-Alsatian creature from The NeverEnding Story? It was probably just a hoarse duck. I'd been spending far too much time on my own lately…

Still stuck in the woods, with the path descending gradually, I kept catching glimpses of a mountain with a dusting of snow but mist masking its summit. It had to be Ben Lomond. I pulled out my map to have this confirmed and also to figure out roughly where I was. By the looks of it, I had passed the twenty-four mile mark on the West Highland Way. Midway through the second morning of my walk and I had already covered a quarter of the ninety-six-mile distance. Reaching this milestone fairly put a spring in my step. This was a piece of cake… so far.

Next thing I knew I was approaching the remote Rowardennan Hotel ('Beneath the Ben' stated a sign), so I nipped inside with the aim of obtaining a mid-morning coffee. The receptionist explained that I would be able to get one in the Clansman bar, which opened at eleven o'clock and had a separate entrance at the side of the hotel. It was ten to eleven now. Deciding that I could afford to hang around for a much-needed shot of caffeine, I wandered back outside and sat down on a bench in the sunshine, waiting for the Clansman to open.

At eleven o'clock on the dot, I entered the bar. 'I hope you're not thinking of going up Ben Lomond,' said the barman, noting my backpack and outdoor clothing.

'Not a chance,' I said, shaking my head. Going up Ben Lomond was the last thing in the world I wanted to do right now. All I wanted was to relax with a coffee before resuming my low-level walk.

The barman explained that, despite the seemingly decent weather, conditions were poor for climbing Ben Lomond, hence the helicopter circling the mountain. I had heard the whirr of rotor blades on my approach to the hotel.

Ben Lomond is the most southerly of Scotland's two-hundred-and-eighty-two Munros and is one of the most popular ones to bag, its proximity to Glasgow ensuring a steady stream of hill-walkers determined to reach its summit.

I explained to the barman that I was simply doing the West Highland Way and that bagging my first Munro was not part of the plan. 'My son ran the West Highland Way in twenty-four hours,' he said, whilst serving my coffee with an Italian biscuit on the side.

'That's amazing,' I said, meaning his son's astonishing achievement and not the free biscuit.

'That's mad,' the barman corrected me, tapping his temple with his index finger to emphasise what he thought of his son running the West Highland Way.

'So how far are you walking today?' he asked me.

'As far as the Drovers Inn,' I replied. The historic inn, just north of Loch Lomond at Inverarnan, was to be my base for the night.

'That's fifteen miles from here,' frowned the barman.

'Then I've already done a third of my distance for today,' I grinned.

He sighed and shook his head. In his eyes, I was no more sensible than his son. I had become one of those Walkers who normal people couldn't get their heads around.

I took a seat with my coffee and once the barman had wandered off somewhere, I removed my shoes and changed my socks. I hadn't yet reached the ten-mile mark but figured this was as good a time as any to make that all-important sock switch for the benefit of my feet.

Once I'd put my shoes back on, I glanced up at the telly on the wall to see Bobby Gillespie from Primal Scream and Super Hans from the TV sitcom Peep Show battling it out in a penalty shootout. I wondered if I should be hallucinating this early in my trip. Having established that this was indeed a genuine event on some football show, I got up from my chair to take to the road again.

'Good luck,' said the barman. 'Only the fifteen miles to go...' I wasn't sure if he was offering me words of encouragement or taking the mickey. Suspecting it to be the latter, I thanked him in any case.

Stepping back outside, I was struck by how much the temperature seemed to have dropped since I was sitting on the bench half-an-hour ago, waiting for the Clansman to open. In the time it had taken me to have a coffee, all that bright sunshine had been replaced by dark clouds. Springtime in Scotland.

According to my map, it would be another eight miles before I reached the next sign of civilisation, the even more remote Inversnaid Hotel. Until then it would just be me, Loch Lomond and the trees... and possibly some feral goats.

I got going again and embarked on a gradual climb along a forest track. The coffee and change of socks seemed to have worked wonders. It was as if I'd pressed the reset button. I felt as fresh as when I had first set out from Balmaha a few hours ago, possibly even better since my heel wasn't giving me any grief. How long, I wondered, until I started to fade and really feel the pain?

Walk This Way

Right now, though, the West Highland Way was offering me a choice. I could carry on climbing among the trees, or switch to an alternative trail which stuck close to the loch shore for a couple of miles until the two paths met up again. I had heard that the low route, while more scenic, was more hard-going and would take longer. Not really wishing to add anything to my day's walk – I'd much rather subtract – I dismissed the loch-side option and put my faith in the forest excursion.

Having taken the high road, I soon discovered that I could see plenty of Loch Lomond anyway due to the bareness of the trees in early springtime. I also noticed that the loch was narrowing, giving the false impression that I was nearing the end of it. Having cycled the length of Loch Lomond plenty of times on the opposite shore, I knew the score. This wasn't over by a long chalk.

On the other side of the water I could see a cluster of buildings. I consulted my map and figured that it was the village of Tarbet. How many Tarbets were there in Scotland? I knew of at least three, with one on the Isle of Harris, although the others were possibly Tarberts rather than Tarbets... I was now talking to myself out loud and decided that I really needed to stop doing that.

After I fell silent, my right thigh started protesting. Was this because I'd sat down for that coffee a short while ago? Whether or not this was the case, my body was definitely complaining. Not loudly but still grumbling. First my left heel, now it was my right thigh. No, wait, the pain in my thigh had just shifted to my knee. This was like a game of pain ping pong, with my body the table.

In terms of my physical surroundings, it had suddenly become much greener in this woodland I was blundering through. Within a few footsteps, it had gone from bare trees to branches covered in leaves. It was as if I had stumbled from winter into summer, skipping spring.

Small waterfalls and rushing streams abounded. With water spilling down the hills on my right and the soothing swish of the loch on my left, it was akin to aquatic surround sound, or being spun around in nature's washing machine. Either way, it was lovely.

Also the forest carpet of moss and pine needles made it pleasingly soft underfoot, with my right leg no longer acting up either. This was a positively beautiful stretch of the West Highland Way, a comforting stroll through woods of birch, oak and pine. The air was cool beneath the canopy of trees and there was still no sign of any other walkers. In fact, the only indication of anyone having been here was a single discarded sock on the path.

Then, descending through the forest a short while later, I bumped into a woman walking in the other direction. 'Everyone seems to be running past me!' she laughed, half out of breath. I hadn't realised I was moving so fast, nor that there were others in front of me.

'I feel so inadequate!' joked the woman who, given that she was tackling the West Highland Way north to south, was a lot closer to her final destination than I was.

'Ach, you're doing fine,' I said, pointing out that a recent cup of coffee was probably the reason for my speed – and that I no doubt would be slowing down shortly.

Soon after this rare encounter with another human being, I emerged from the woods and found myself back on the loch shore. While I had bumped into a fellow walker, I was yet to meet any of Loch Lomond's feral goats and wasn't sure I wanted to. My only wildlife sightings so far had been those ducks back at Balmaha and, more recently, two beetles crossing the path in front of me. The big challenge would come when I witnessed a bird of prey – or pretty much any bird for that matter – for I would have real trouble identifying it. I could tell a seagull from a pigeon but that was about it as far as differentiating between bird species went. Although I also knew what a robin looked like... I'd seen them on Christmas cards.

After crossing a burn, I passed a Hansel and Gretel cottage with a smoking chimney, and happened upon the second 'honesty' tuck shop of my travels so far. A lovely handwritten sign read 'A Wee Treat To Help Along The Way' and I checked to see what delights were on offer for the weary traveller. 'Home-made cookies' sounded tempting but I plumped for 'Granny's special recipe traditional Scottish tablet'.

I took a small bag of this much-trumpeted tablet from the Tupperware box and put a pound coin in the padlocked tin. Then I turned the tap of a large glass dispenser that contained water and lemons – a nice and unexpected offering – and filled my bottle. It seemed that everywhere you went on the Way, people were looking out for you.

Marching along while munching on some of Granny's delicious tablet, I was soon wincing. Not because I had done untold damage to my teeth but due to the unwelcome return of the pain in my left heel. There was always something to take the edge off the happiness.

As before, the pain subsided. Until the path itself started giving me a headache... Although it remained close to the shoreline, I was having to clamber over tree roots and boulders. It was just as my friend Martin had described it – but still it threw me.

During one particularly rocky sequence of this loch-side obstacle course, I found myself having to use my hands to scramble around. This wasn't walking. I had little patience for this monkey business and it wasn't long before I was officially fed up with Loch Lomond and its bonnie, bonnie banks. Blasted, gnarly banks, more like.

After negotiating another tricky section, I was met with a loud 'Hiya!' from a woman heading towards me. She was positively bounding along and seemed unreasonably cheery, given the vexing nature of the so-called path. I greeted her in return, putting on a smile in a failed attempt to not look too flustered.

Minutes after she had gone on her merry way, I was faced with the frankly terrifying prospect of having to cross a narrow ledge with perhaps a fifteen-feet drop to the loch below. You'd think the woman might have mentioned the ledge? But no. She'd no doubt skipped across it whilst whistling a tune. I did the exact opposite, negotiating the ledge – barely wider than my foot – in grim silence. I edged towards the other side, not daring to look down, all too aware that the slightest slip would land me in the loch. Honestly, I couldn't take much more of this high drama. Who did the planners of the West Highland Way think I was? Indiana flipping Jones?

When I eventually made it across the Ledge of Doom – those half-dozen hesitant steps seemed to take an eternity – I breathed a loch-sized sigh of relief.

Having survived this unexpected trial, I reached for my bottle and gulped down some of that sweet lemon water. I really hoped there would be no more nasty surprises requiring me to be a daredevil when I was nothing but a scaredy-cat.

Pressing on and trying to forget about the trauma of the ludicrous ledge, I came to a seriously muddy section that put me in mind of the Swamp of Sadness in The NeverEnding Story. The Swamp of Sadness was where the boy-warrior Atreyu's beloved horse Artax perished in a heart-breaking scene. I didn't have a horse. Nor was I the hero in an Eighties fantasy movie (something I kept having to remind myself).

Once I'd successfully made it through the mud – feeling thankful for the indestructible walking shoes sold to me by my outdoor guru John – the strangest thing happened… I broke into a jog. I soon put a stop to that nonsense, reverting to a more sensible pace as I strained my ears to hear the commentary coming from a tourist boat out on the loch. The sizeable vessel was fairly close to the shore and the chat from the tour guide was being relayed through loudspeakers, but I still couldn't quite make out what the holidaymakers were being told about their immediate surroundings.

I imagined it was something along the lines of [adopts David Attenborough voice] 'and there… scurrying among the trees… is the West Highland Way Walker… a solitary creature with a skin of Gore-Tex… whose main source of nourishment is Granny's traditional Scottish tablet…'

While the tourists were no doubt thrilled to have caught a glimpse of me in action, and were probably busy snapping away with their cameras so that they could wow friends and family back home, I was even more ecstatic when I spotted a large building up ahead. It had to be the Inversnaid Hotel. Civilisation!

Such was my excitement that I started jogging again, only slowing down when I came to an impressive waterfall right next to the hotel. I paused to take a couple of pictures… just as the heavens opened. Realising that I was photographing water while being drenched in the stuff, I stopped capturing the waterfall and dived into the hotel, making a beeline for the bar. I asked the barmaid for a cup of coffee and a glass of water. Then substituted the coffee for a pint of beer. I didn't bother ordering any food as I hadn't long scoffed the tuna roll in my bag, along with the Mars bar. And still I had some oatcakes and a banana in reserve, as well as a few last chunks of Granny's special tablet.

'I take it you're doing the West Highland Way,' said the barmaid, pouring my pint.

'Aye,' I replied. 'That last part was pretty scary. I had to walk across a ledge!'

'Where are you heading for today?' she asked. Clearly my hair-raising encounter with the Ledge of Doom was of little interest to her.

'Inverarnan,' I said. 'I'm staying at the Drovers Inn.'

'Well,' she smiled, handing me my beer, 'enjoy your pint because the next part is supposed to be the hardest.'

'What, the walk between here and Inverarnan?'

'I'm afraid so,' she nodded. 'That's what everyone says.'

Trying not to look too panicked, I took my beer and water, and went and hid in a dark corner of the bar. Maybe I could enquire about a room and hole up here for the night then pick up the trail again tomorrow?

My watch beeped to remind me that I still hadn't bothered to figure out how to stop it going off every hour. It was already three o'clock and I still had seven miles to go. Seven gruelling miles by the sound of it. I wasn't enjoying this pint one bit. I sighed and stood up. There was no point in putting this off any longer.

On my way out of the hotel, I bumped into another walker in the lobby. Tall and skinny, he was tilting forward slightly due to his giant backpack and had been soaked by the rain. His name was Lucas and he was from Belgium. Obviously. A weary and hungry Lucas was looking to sit down and have a bite to eat before continuing his journey northwards. I told him that I was heading for Inverarnan.

'I don't know if I'll make it that far at this time of day,' he sighed. 'It's four hours...'

I was actually hoping to do it in closer to two hours, despite the apparent difficulty of these seven miles. Was I kidding myself? Well, there was no way I was waiting on Lucas... he probably didn't even want me to wait for him. What was The Walkers' Code? Should I at least offer to hang around? Were we in this together, or was it every man for himself? My dilemma was solved by a famished Lucas wishing me 'good luck' and staggering off in the direction of the bar.

With no one left to talk to, I resumed my trek under thick clouds. Luckily the rain had stopped but there was a nagging sense that the day was running away from me. The loch-side path was straightforward initially, nothing out of the ordinary. Perhaps I had nothing to worry about... besides the feral goats.

Then I met them.

Rounding a corner, I caught sight of a jet-black creature up ahead in the long grass. A panther! At least that was my initial reaction. Then I noticed that it had horns, which ruled out the possibility of it being a panther. This animal was also rather on the small side. Nope, it was a feral goat.

At least it wasn't charging towards me. Although it was staring at me and perhaps thinking of charging towards me. I then spotted another goat... and another... I counted at least a dozen of the horned critters. Some of them were eyeballing me, others were simply ignoring me. Then the tiniest goat stumbled out of the long grass and onto the path in front of me. I wasn't quite sure what to do. I slowed down so as not to frighten it and, more to the point, not to annoy Mummy or Daddy goat. Then one of the bigger goats (Mum, Dad, Uncle Clarence?) acted, ushering the kid off the path and back into the long grass. They were making way for me. What a considerate bunch of goats!

Shortly after that encounter with my feral friends, I was surprised by a procession of people marching towards me, a battalion of youngsters with hefty backpacks and big beams on their faces. They looked so happy and healthy and as they passed by me they all cried 'Hi!' as if this was quite simply The Best Day Ever. These alarmingly upbeat souls – judging by their accents – were young Americans.

Given that they were pressing southwards, they must have been fresh from tackling what was billed to be the toughest part of the West Highland Way. Maybe I really did have nothing to be concerned about. But then again, these shiny, happy people were Americans who, in my experience, were relentlessly cheery. They could have been walking for three days straight without a wink of sleep and still been off the scale in terms of sheer joyousness.

Certainly their sunny mood was out of step with the dreich Scottish weather. Really it would have been far better if I had bumped into a group of grumpy natives muttering and cursing about having just gone through hell. At least then I would have known where I stood and what I was in for.

Because I soon knew all about it as I took a walk on the wild side... The first troublesome section required some scrambling on my behalf and after that it just got silly. Boulders to the left of me, boulders to the right, here I was stuck in the middle of a major obstacle course.

I struggled to squeeze between one rock and a tree and, at one point, found myself hanging from a branch just to stay upright. More monkey business. Then I slipped on a tree root but thankfully landed safely. Some of this was ankle-twisting territory. Hearing the noise of a motor, I turned to face the loch and saw someone jet-skiing across the water. It was quite clear that they were having more fun than me.

Having negotiated another mad up-and-down scramble in complicated terrain, I was then accosted by an army of tiny flying insects. They couldn't be midges, could they? It was still March and I'd been led to believe that there wouldn't be any. This wasn't in the contract...

Struggling along the 'path', waging war with badly situated boulders and triptastic tree roots, it took me the best part of an hour to advance one measly mile. Progress was painfully slow and I felt bone-weary. This was illustrated perfectly when, staggering around in an uncoordinated manner, I accidentally shoulder-barged a tree. My shoulder came off worse.

Up ahead I could see a solitary tiny island in the middle of the loch. I consulted my map and learned that it was the curiously named Island I Vow – as I vowed never to come here again. I also noted from my map that I'd missed the detour to Rob Roy's Cave. He probably wasn't in anyway.

After what felt like forever the terrain became less of a headache as I began to pick up the pace on a path that was approaching normal. Apart from when it all went a bit Indiana Jones again, with me having to climb up some steep steps in front of a waterfall and cross a rickety bridge. At least it wasn't a ludicrous ledge.

A little later, I passed another waterfall and barely gave it a glance. I was getting fairly blasé about water spectacles. Knowing that I was finally making decent progress, I decided to take a breather and sat down on a tree stump to demolish the banana that had been lying in my bag since early morning. While munching on my banana, my ears picked up the distant music of what sounded like an ice cream van. Surely I was hearing things. There was no way I was even remotely close to a single nougat wafer.

I felt like giving myself a slap in the face but instead changed my socks again. There was no real need for a second switch of the day but I viewed it as a timely boost ahead of the remaining few miles. Whether it was as a result of the second change of socks or not, I began jogging once more on an easier stretch. Even on the stonier parts, I found myself springing from rock to rock like a human mountain goat in the making. Much more of these athletic antics and I really would turn into a mountain goat, never to return to my wife and family.

When I came to a gate, I greeted it with a grin because this signalled the end of my loch-side torture. No longer would I be getting in a dreadful fankle on those boulder-strewn wooded slopes that had made the past couple of hours total misery. As I stood on a gravel bay looking back down Loch Lomond, I felt a mixture of relief and a sense of achievement. I had developed a love-hate relationship with lochs. I loved seeing the back of them and hated what they put me through.

Turning away from the water, I pressed on through some trees and reached a section of open ground where it became so muddy at one point that I misread the path and ended up circling a sodden field. Not exactly my idea of fun but still more enjoyable than Loch Lomond.

Crossing a burn at least gave me the chance to lose some of the mud from my boots but I was then less than amused when I discovered that I still had one more climb on my hands. Up I went on a stony path to reach the crest of a col where I promptly sat down to take in the raised views back down Loch Lomond (good riddance) and north to some menacing mountains beneath dark clouds (oh for God's sake). Feeling hungry, I delved into my bag and pulled out the only remaining edible items: oatcakes. I started scoffing them and, as my mouth dried up, I realised to my horror that I was out of water. I made that fourth oatcake my last but was still worried that my reckless feasting would be my undoing and that I'd suffer death by oatcakes.

Still surviving, I stumbled down into Glen Falloch for the leisurely finale to a trying day. After crossing a stream by stepping stones, I came to a campsite complete with wigwams and a pub. Two men stood outside the pub smoking. They were wearing identical T-shirts with 'The Way' printed on the back and were chatting to a woman whose own T-shirt bore the slogan 'Get Spooked at the Drovers Inn'.

Ah yes. The Drovers Inn – where I was staying – was supposed to be haunted. But then I wouldn't actually be sleeping in the eighteenth-century inn itself. Due to the presence of a film crew, all guests were being housed in more modern lodgings across the road. I had received an email explaining the situation along with the offer of a complimentary bottle of wine to make up for any inconvenience caused.

It wasn't putting me out any, not staying in a haunted old inn. All I wanted was a bed and the guarantee of a good night's sleep uninterrupted by paranormal activities. Unless the ghosts of the Drovers Inn were going to float across the road in the middle of the night just to upset me... I'd sleep with the lights on.

After crossing a bridge, I walked on a path by the side of the road towards the inn. A minibus sped past with 'Baggage Transfer' emblazoned on its side. It was possible to have your bag transported between your accommodation for a small fee, allowing you to walk the West Highland

Way free of any burden. This seemed like cheating to me. Although hardcore campers might level that accusation at softies like myself for choosing a bed over a tent. Each to their own, I supposed.

As I approached the Drovers Inn, the film crew were busy packing up and loading various pieces of equipment into trucks. There went my chances of being an extra in a Hollywood blockbuster. I thought about trying to collar the producer and pitching Gary Sutherland and the Ledge of Doom as it had all the makings of a box-office hit. Although of course I would insist on a stunt double for the ledge in question because there was no way I was putting myself through all that again.

I picked up my key at reception and got settled in my room at the lodge across the road before returning to the Drovers Inn for dinner in the cosy bar, which despite the film shoot remained open to the public. I tucked into a plate of scampi and chips and also made a sizeable dent in my complimentary bottle of red wine... well, I had walked twenty-two miles, with Loch bloody Lomond taking up the bulk of them.

While the bar was rather quiet, the hallway was packed. With wild animals. Wolves, various birds of prey and a fearsome bear poised by the doorway. The Drovers Inn was heavy on the taxidermy.

I turned in for an early night and did not receive any visitations from spectres. But I did have a bad dream about being chased by a bear through woods and having to leap from a ledge into a loch in order to escape a savaging.

— Day Three
West Highland Way
Inverarnan to Inveroran
Twenty-two miles

The A to B on day three was slightly confusing: Inverarnan to Inveroran. On paper, it almost looked as if I wasn't going anywhere. The reality, however, was a twenty-two-mile trek between two similarly spelt places. No rest for the walker!

After a substantial cooked breakfast – no haggis on this occasion but black pudding aplenty – I hit the Way again, following the lively River Falloch with its rocky rapids and cascades. The show was over all too soon as the river calmed down. But there was then a dramatic change in the landscape as Glen Falloch opened up and I strode between its moorland flanks. This was classic Highland scenery. It was what I had imagined the West Highland Way to be. Everything was golden, too, in the morning sunshine, while the walking itself was a pleasure after the painfully slow progress up Loch Lomond's shore.

I soon encountered a father and son, Mike and Jonathan, in matching red woolly hats and sturdy boots. They had driven up from London for some mountain adventures.

'We'll be walking until just where the snow starts,' explained Mike cheerily. This was his teenage son's first time in Scotland. Jonathan had been raised on Dad's tales of the Scottish hills and was about to experience it all first-hand.

'And what about you?' asked Mike.

I said that I was doing the West Highland Way and that I was aiming for Inveroran before crossing Rannoch Moor tomorrow.

'I've driven by Rannoch Moor a few times… it's bleak,'

said Mike. Bleak was the only way I'd ever heard anyone describe Rannoch Moor.

After ten minutes of walking and chatting with Mike and Jonathan, it was time for them to leave me and set about tackling more challenging terrain. I had enjoyed the short spell in their company. It had really given me an early-morning boost.

Forging ahead on my lonesome, I crossed a bridge and continued along the west bank of the River Falloch. After a while, the path left the river and I enjoyed the novelty of passing under a railway line via a low-roofed cattle creep. It had me bent over but at least I didn't become lodged in the tiny tunnel with a giant backpack.

I then marched on uphill – and upright – to join an old military road. Much of the West Highland Way from here onwards followed roads that were constructed in the eighteenth century by government troops to keep the turbulent Highlands in order and prevent further rebellions in the wake of the Jacobite risings. They were built under the command of Major General George Wade and latterly his successor Major William Caulfeild.

From the old military road which I was currently trudging along, I could see the Crianlarich hills and my eyes were mainly drawn to the steep pyramid of Ben More. The 'big ben' is Britain's fifteenth highest mountain and I was quite content to admire it from a distance. Though I was not so happy when, approaching a farm, I encountered my first hitch of the day.

The path in front of me, for the next hundred yards or so, had dissolved into a mud bath. Not just any old mud bath but one plastered with massive cowpats. Recent heavy rain and cattle had clearly combined to devastating effect.

Surveying this apocalyptic scene, I could see no way

round the problem. Hemmed in by a stone dyke on one side and a steep bank on the other, my only option was to attempt to plot a path through the mire by targeting the occasional small rock that had not been submerged in the muck. However, these potential stepping stones were few and far between and some of them would require a real leap of faith. One wrong move and I'd be on my backside in the mud. Or worse still, face down in a cowpat.

It occurred to me that Gordon Burns had really missed a trick by not incorporating a dung-filled mud bath in the obstacle course in The Krypton Factor. The brightly coloured tracksuits of those brainy contestants would have ended up caked in filth, which would have made for even more absorbing 1980s television.

Not wearing a brightly coloured tracksuit and sadly lacking the Krypton Factor, I took a first hesitant step and secured a foot on a stone. Swaying about on one leg, with my backpack not exactly aiding my balance, I stretched out my arms like Daniel in The Karate Kid in an attempt to maintain some equilibrium whilst being marooned in this sea of sludge.

I really hoped the farmer wasn't staring out of his window at me because I must have looked ridiculous. Although this was all his fault anyway. He had no control over the weather but it was his cows that had made an almighty mess of the West Highland Way. At least there were no cows here now because having to negotiate a mud bath full of cowpats and cows would have simply sent me over the edge. The truth is, I was still dealing with the trauma of being chased across a field by that cow many years ago in my Moray childhood.

Lowering my arms and breaking away from the Karate Kid stance, I leapt in a bold bid to reach a second stone and just missed it, sinking into the slime up to my shins. At least

I wasn't knee deep in the ooze and hadn't yet suffered the indignity of landing on a cowpat.

With the next available stone looking pretty much unreachable, I abandoned the stepping-stones tactic and basically dragged myself through the mud, eventually emerging on terra firma as the least convincing swamp creature from a B movie ever.

The lower half of my walking trousers were in an appalling state while I couldn't even see my shoes, so coated were they in sludge. I stumbled on regardless as the mud quickly hardened in the sunshine.

I was still feeling sorry for myself when I bumped into a mother and son striding in the other direction. The mum wanted to know how long it was to Inverarnan. I was the perfect person to ask since I had set out from there. I checked my watch and confirmed that I had left two hours ago.

Her little boy then piped up 'be careful mister, there's a bog back there,' whilst pointing over his shoulder.

'Yes,' said Mum. 'Oscar and I have just come through a really muddy bit.'

'So have I,' I nodded. 'It's pretty bad.'

We commiserated with each other on our muck-themed plights and then went our separate ways as I steeled myself for another slimy episode. Except that it turned out to be not so bad. Certainly nothing like the cataclysmic quagmire I had endured back at the farm. Poor Oscar… I pictured him sunk up to his knees with his mum trying to unplug him from the muck. I hoped they were okay.

Frankly, though, I had myself to worry about and I didn't exactly help my cause when, after entering a forest, I was faced with a fork in the path. The West Highland Way carried on uphill while the other track led down to the village of Crianlarich. It didn't look far on my map and indeed a sign in front of me, advertising the village shop, seemed to confirm the proximity of the place. 'NOT LONG NOW.'

Hmm. I was almost out of water and all that remained food-wise were a couple of oatcakes. It was another six miles to Tyndrum, the next village directly on the route. So it was that I temporarily left the Way and started pacing down the woodland path towards Crianlarich.

The fact that I was heading downhill bothered me a little because it meant that I would have to come back uphill. At least we weren't talking any great distance... After ten minutes had elapsed and still there was no sight of Crianlarich, my mounting concern turned to outright frustration. This was taking flipping ages! My only response was to break into a jog even though I knew I was wasting valuable energy, whilst making no further progress on the actual West Highland Way.

After what felt like an eternity, I emerged from the trees and found myself looking down on a major road, with what appeared to be Crianlarich visible on the other side. My proposed pit stop was reachable via an underpass but, by my reckoning, it would be several more minutes before I even set foot in the village shop (NOT LONG NOW) and I'd already been absent from the West Highland Way for at least fifteen minutes.

If I persisted with this plan of action then my quick detour from the Way might end up costing me the best part of an hour. This was madness. Glowering at the rooftops in the distance, I was by now absolutely livid. And in a fit of pique I turned my back on Crianlarich and started stomping back up the forest track in order to reconnect with the West Highland Way as quickly as possible.

Retracing my steps on an inconvenient but inevitable incline, I was now twice as tired (and ten times as flustered) as when I had first strayed from the official path. I still lacked food and water and wouldn't be able to replenish my near non-existent supplies for at least a couple of hours.

My initial decision to divert to Crianlarich may have felt like a major mistake but my impulsive act of turning around when I was almost there was surely irrational? I was currently facing my biggest struggle since the twisted shores of Loch Lomond and, once more, the battle was mainly being played out in my mind. Physically, I was equipped to cope with this setback but my head was all over the place.

When I finally returned to the point where I had veered off the Way, I plonked myself down on a bench. A bench I should have sat down on half-an-hour ago for a few minutes' rest before carrying on – instead of taking the crackpot decision to head for Crianlarich, which I vowed to never visit again despite having not quite been there.

Lying back on the bench, I closed my eyes for a moment and tried to compose myself while a helicopter circled overhead. Perhaps if I waved, they might winch down some water? But then a parched walker probably wasn't classed as an emergency. I made do with the tiniest of sips from my near-empty water bottle (there were two more sips left at most) then rose from the bench to resume the West Highland Way.

It was cool in the shade of the forest and this at least helped keep my thirst at bay. But I wasn't taking in my surroundings much. I was on autopilot, stuck in a dream-like state. Dehydrated, basically. My mouth was dry and I had a mind full of regret... that botched attempt to reach Crianlarich had added a pointless mile to the twenty two I was already tasked with walking.

Walk This Way

An extended downhill stretch through the woods raised my spirits a little, although it occurred to me that this welcome descent would have been even better on a bike. When I reached a footbridge straddling a burn, I sat down, changed my socks and took the second-last sip of my water.

Stumbling on, I became quite disorientated when the path ducked beneath a viaduct and I found myself hemmed in between the railway line and the A82. I then realised that I needed to cross the road, a task which required my total attention and quickly brought me back to my senses.

Once safely across the road, I climbed over a stile and walked next to fields of sheep until I reached a bridge spanning the River Fillan. I stopped to take in the splendid view south across the plain to the snow-capped Crianlarich hills – and then checked both my map and my watch.

It appeared to be the case that, in the wake of the Crianlarich calamity, I had covered the last three miles in three-quarters-of-an-hour, some of my speediest progress yet. Clearly the key to this long-distance walking lark was to become angry with yourself and not drink any water.

I continued past a farm, drawing the attention of barking dogs, and then passed the ruins of an old priory before a sign for a farm shop (promising coffee, cold drinks and bacon rolls!) had me in raptures. I wouldn't have to wait until Tyndrum to quench my thirst and satisfy my hunger. Lunch was happening now!

I ran into the farm shop and grabbed a two-litre bottle of water and a can of Coke from the fridge then rushed to the counter where I ordered a black coffee and asked if I could have a roll and sausage. The man nodded and replied: 'We've got sausage, we've got bacon, we've got egg, we've got sausage and egg, bacon and egg, bacon and sausage...' He had exhausted all the possibilities. Apart from sausage, bacon and egg. I stuck with a roll and sausage and, while it was being prepared, had another look round the shop. Some of the contents of the freezers surprised me. Besides packs of beef, pork and lamb, they had zebra, impala, camel, shark, llama, wildebeest… all manner of exotic meats.

Once I had my roll and sausage in my hands, I took it outside and devoured it after sinking the can of Coke in a oner. Best meal of the trip so far, without a doubt. It was all about context. My thirst had been sated and my hunger dealt with, plus the sun was shining and I had a grand view of mountains to the north.

While I sat on a bench, sipping my coffee and feeling fully revitalised, a woman came and joined me. She wore the biggest backpack I'd seen yet on my travels and, after a brief struggle, she managed to free it from her shoulders and drop it at her feet. Margaret, who was Scottish and not remotely Belgian, sat down with a sigh and nodded towards her humongous bag. 'The thing is,' she laughed, 'there's nothing in there I don't need!'

Margaret was mainly camping along the Way – hence tent, pots and pans – but had spent last night at a bunkhouse. 'A man from one of the baggage transfer services turned up at the bunkhouse this morning and said he could take my bag for £10 if I wanted,' said Margaret. 'He picked it up and asked: "What have you got in there?!" And I told him that everything in there was vital to me. Camping gear, cooking equipment, clothes… I didn't take him up on the offer but I might need to have a rethink about baggage transfers at some point. We'll see how it goes. Did you get something to eat here?'

I told Margaret that I'd just had a roll and sausage and that it was mighty tasty. 'Ooh, I might have to get one of those,' she said. 'Do they have bottles of water?'

'Yep,' I said, picking up my two-litre job.

'Don't think I need one of those,' joked Margaret, indicating her colossal backpack. 'I'm not sure I could carry the extra weight.'

We were then joined by a young French couple, Florent and Catherine, who were also doing the West Highland Way and whose backpacks were substantial in size but not quite on the same scale as Margaret's. I asked them how they were faring.

'We are doing good,' said Catherine, 'but we are starting to slow down.'

'At least the weather is not terrible,' smiled Florent.

I wanted to stay and chat some more with my fellow walkers but needed to be getting a move on. I still had nine more miles ahead of me and wanted to reach Inveroran at a decent hour, so that I could rest up properly ahead of tomorrow's no doubt arduous trek across Rannoch Moor. So I said cheerio to Margaret, Florent and Catherine and started making tracks for Tyndrum. Even though the sun was still shining, the temperature seemed to have plummeted all of a sudden and, for the first time, I felt like putting on my gloves.

Walking along the banks of the River Fillan, I was startled by the sight of an elegantly dressed lady riding towards me on a white horse. 'Lovely day!' she smiled as she rode by. I replied that it was indeed a lovely day (even if it was flipping freezing).

Shortly afterwards I passed a sign saying: 'Artisan cafe three minutes walk'. I had to admit I was sceptical – not of the cafe's artisan credentials but the claimed walking distance. After that recent caper trying to reach the village shop in Crianlarich, I was naturally suspicious that the owners of this artisan cafe may have craftily shaved a few minutes off the actual distance in order to lure walkers from the main path. In any case, I'd not long had my lunch, so there was absolutely no need for another detour.

Still wandering beside the riverbank, I encountered a lively collie dog whose owner was perched on a rock in the middle of the river, holding a fishing rod. The man gave me a nod and I waved in return as I strolled on, while continuing to enjoy the low-key pleasantness of my surroundings.

As I closed in on Tyndrum, the Way turned away from the river and took me through sparse woodland before I stumbled upon a peaty lochan and a stone bench that bore the inscription: 'The Loch of the Legend of the Lost Sword'. I sat down on the bench to catch my breath, collect my thoughts and gaze at the round pool of dark water, which was the colour of stewed tea.

Legend has it that 'The Loch of the Legend of the Lost Sword' was where Robert the Bruce threw his weapon as he and his remaining men fled following defeat to the Clan MacDougall in the Battle of Dalrigh in 1306. Bruce's sword was reputed to have been nine-feet long... but I still couldn't see it sticking out of the lochan.

Half an hour later, I was seated in a cafe in Tyndrum, scoffing cake and staring out the window at the chaffinches. On the other side of the glass was a bird feeding station. I knew they were chaffinches thanks to the helpful bird chart pinned up on the wall next to me. Taking my eye off the chaffinches, I glanced around the cafe. It was pretty busy but I estimated that there was at least ten feet between me and the nearest customer. A safe enough distance for me to remove my shoes and air my feet without fear of causing major offence.

Cake devoured and shoes back on, I resumed my journey. On my way out of Tyndrum, I passed 'The Last

Shop Before Kinlochleven' but opted not to stock up on supplies. I was counting on the two hotels that I would be staying at between now and Kinlochleven to sort me out in the food stakes. Whether this was a foolhardy decision or not, I'd find out soon enough. Not long after I'd shunned the opportunity to get some shopping in, I spied another walker up ahead as the Way climbed on a steep-sided pass through to Glen Orchy. The man wore a giant backpack and appeared to be walking with some difficulty. As I caught up with him, I realised that he was on the phone. He gave me a nod and whispered to me: 'Just a minute'. After he had finished his call, he offered me his hand and introduced himself as Andy.

He had been phoning a friend for some much-needed moral support. As I'd suspected, he was having a hard time of it. The root of Andy's problem was the current state of his feet. A Scotsman living and working down south, he had decided to do the West Highland Way at the last minute and had driven up from England, buying a bunch of walking gear from an outdoor shop in Gretna. Andy hadn't had time to break in his new boots, plus they weren't the perfect fit he had thought when trying them on in the shop. He was currently walking gingerly on account of two rather large blisters.

'I've also got a sore knee,' winced Andy, my sympathy for him increasing by the second. 'Going uphill isn't so bad. It's when I go downhill I get this shooting pain. Between the dodgy knee and the blisters, I'm not in the best shape right now!'

To compound his discomfort, Andy was also struggling with a hangover. He too had stayed at the Drovers last night and had hit the bar late on with three pals, who had driven up from Glasgow for a catch-up at the end of his second day on the Way. So Andy had wound up having four drinks. 'Two pints, a whisky and a brandy.' He'd fallen victim to the Having To Get Your Round In rule. Four friends couldn't just go for the one drink in Scotland. Or two or even three. Four was the minimum requirement.

'Aye, but I don't think whisky was a good idea,' groaned Andy. 'That brandy wasn't too clever either...'

On a more positive note, his load had been lightened by his mates taking his tent back with them to Glasgow. He'd had great intentions of camping most nights but the pain of his early progress had made him take the executive decision to ditch the tent and stay at hotels, thus making his journey just that little bit more bearable.

Like me, Andy was walking the West Highland Way over five days. Even though he was clearly in some discomfort and was still carrying a fairly heavy load, I had faith in him that he would complete his journey. He may not have been moving too freely but he had a steely determination about him. Andy was also, despite his current hardships, enjoying the abundance of fresh air and first-class scenery.

The two of us were walking beneath the steep western flank of Beinn Odhar and Andy expressed a degree of sympathy for a mountain that fell just forty feet short of being a Munro. It did at least have the small consolation of being a Corbett. Off to our left was the railway track of the much-celebrated West Highland Line and when a southbound train came into view, Andy grabbed his phone to take a picture.

'I'm not a trainspotter – but I do work on the trains!' he explained. 'This is to show the guys at work.'

Andy was a train driver and wanted to give his rail colleagues in England a flavour of the kind of dramatic landscapes that some of their northern counterparts had the regular pleasure of passing through. As we progressed – more at Andy's pace than mine – the cone-shaped Beinn Dorain (most definitely a Munro) soared into view, with its sweeping, grassy slope and a touch of snow decorating its summit. Andy and I marvelled at the dominating presence of this majestic mountain. For me, it was by some margin the visual highlight of the West Highland Way so far.

'You should head on,' said Andy, still walking gingerly and aware that he was slowing me down. I honestly didn't mind as I was enjoying his company. But I still had seven miles to go to Inveroran whereas Andy's more modest aim was to reach Bridge of Orchy – a few miles closer – in one piece and rest up there for the night. And so I expressed the hope that his feet would hold up and said cheerio to the bold Andy. I also hoped our paths might cross again before we reached Fort William, although I imagined this was unlikely. I pressed on, glancing back from time to time and seeing the blue-jacketed Andy become smaller and smaller until I could make him out no longer.

Meanwhile, Beinn Dorain kept getting bigger and bigger until I was at the foot of the mountain and began walking along its base for what seemed like forever. Every time I looked up, there it was, looming above me and making me feel like a mere speck on the landscape, which I was.

At one point, I sat down on a grassy bank to give my feet a rest and eat something. Pulling an oatcake from my bag, I actually said out loud: 'Right, let's be having you'. This was the danger of spending too much time on your own. You ended up talking to biscuits. I wished that Andy was around to keep me sane…

Gazing north, I could see dark mountains with black clouds hanging over them, a menacing sight that put me in mind of Mordor. I guessed I was heading that way tomorrow. Hopefully, it would be sunnier.

When I eventually reached tiny Bridge of Orchy a short while later, I popped into the Bridge of Orchy Hotel. It was almost teatime and I still had three more miles to walk but I felt as though I was due some sort of reward for my afternoon's efforts. So I ordered a pint of ale (the reward), a pint of water (necessary) and a packet of prawn cocktail crisps (nutrition) then sat down in a corner of the bar.

A group of outdoor types at the next table were all kicking back with their shoes off. Since it seemed to be the done thing, I decided to follow suit. I then gulped down half of my pint of water and tipped the rest, along with the wedge of lemon, into my water bottle, so that I could tackle those final few miles to Inveroran in style.

Turning my attention to the beer and crisps, I was half hoping that Andy might turn up, so that I could congratulate him on making it to Bridge of Orchy with his sore feet. But then I'd end up buying him a pint and he'd insist on buying me one back – as per the rules – and before I knew it I would have necked three pints, with still some walking to do. Nope, it was best that he wasn't here really…

Stepping out of the hotel and into the early evening sunshine, I crossed an old bridge over the River Orchy and followed the waymarked path as it zigzagged up through a forestry plantation and onto open moorland for a panoramic view that took my breath away (though I was still able to swear in astonishment). I could see for miles around and looked back to Beinn Dorain as well as ahead to Loch Tulla below me and mountains beyond.

After spending a few moments stationary and in an awestruck state, I got my tired legs moving again and headed down the hill towards the isolated Inveroran Hotel. I was caught in a sudden sun shower as I descended to my white-washed haven in the heart of wild country. The drenched and bedraggled figure that staggered into the hotel, dripping rainwater on the lobby carpet, still received a warm welcome. I was given my room key by my host Koa and presented with the evening menu. Tonight's meal – with all dishes cooked by Koa's wife Nadia – was clearly going to be several steps up in quality from what I was accustomed to. Less roll and sausage, and more starter of smoked salmon followed by medallions of venison. The price of this mouth-watering fare seemed very reasonable too. I thought I would skip pudding and perhaps round off my meal with a dram. Yep, I was going to treat myself tonight... ahead of my certain suffering on Rannoch Moor tomorrow.

After a hot bath, I made good use of the tea-and-coffee-making facilities and tucked into some of the complimentary shortbread. The rest of the shortbread went in my bag as, at some point tomorrow out on the moor, a sudden overload of butter and sugar might be just the thing I needed. I then headed downstairs for dinner. The hotel had a perfectly nice dining room but I chose to eat in the cosy walkers' bar.

'There's usually a good crack in there,' Koa had said when I was checking in. He turned out not to be wrong on that front. After I had polished off my plates of salmon and venison, the tiny bar began to fill up. The first person I got chatting to was Kurt, a young German from Munich, who explained that the first thing he had done after landing in Scotland was to go and climb Ben Lomond. He had then picked up the West Highland Way at Rowardennan and would be seeing it through to its conclusion in Fort William. After that, Skye was on the cards.

'It's the highlight of my trip,' said Kurt.

And after Skye?

'No exact plans,' he shrugged. 'I have three weeks to explore.' Kurt's Scotland trip was a mixture of the not-to-be-missed and the spontaneous.

We compared notes on our West Highland Way experiences so far before Kurt headed off for an early night, just as two other men entered the bar. One of them headed straight to the counter to order a couple of pints while his pal went to sit down in a corner and bumped his head off a lower section of ceiling in the process.

'I always do that,' he groaned, rubbing his head. 'That's the second time today.'

The man with the sore head introduced himself as Dean. He was from Derby, as was his friend Steve, now making his way back from the bar carrying two pints and being extra careful not to bang his own head off the low area of ceiling and cause any unwanted spillages of precious lager. Dean and Steve were doing the West Highland Way and had pitched their tent within a short walking distance of the hotel. The pair of them were actually West Highland Way veterans. This was Dean's sixth time while Steve was only one trek behind his regular walking companion.

'Some of my friends, who prefer the warmth of the Mediterranean, don't understand,' shrugged Steve, taking a sip of his pint.

The first time they tackled the West Highland Way together was back in 2008.

'It was the middle of summer and we had the worst week of weather,' laughed Dean. 'Streams of water coming down the Devil's Staircase...'

Yet the next time they did it, in April, they were able to walk all the way to Fort William in shorts and T-shirt.

'Every morning we unzipped the tent to clear blue skies,' smiled Steve. 'I thought then: "We'll never have this again".'

'But we keep coming back,' said Dean, who, closer to home, enjoyed walking in the Peak District and had done all two-hundred-and-sixty-seven miles of the Pennine Way from deepest Derbyshire to the Scottish Borders.

They asked how I was getting on and I told them that this was my first time doing anything like this. I mentioned the troublesome Loch Lomond section and Steve nodded: 'Pain in the arse'.

'It's a bloody obstacle course,' said Dean.

We compared mileages. They had started their day in Crianlarich and were taking their time, spreading the journey over the course of a week. I explained that I had set out from Inverarnan first thing and that I had covered similar distances of twenty-odd miles in my previous two days.

'That's hardcore,' said Dean, raising his pint glass. 'I'm impressed.'

'We've had a few nights in this place over the years,' grinned Steve, gazing around the walkers' bar in a contented manner.

'I always end up drunk when I'm in here,' sighed Dean.

'Remember that night we got merry with a bunch of Belgians?' laughed Steve.

'Belgians?' I asked. They were everywhere.

Whilst I was busy telling Dean and Steve about the baffling number of Belgians I'd bumped into on my travels so far, two more guys wandered into the tiny bar, pretty much filling the place.

They weren't Belgian. They were Jimmy and Dougie, from Edinburgh and Glasgow respectively.

'East meets west!' joked Dean.

Jimmy and Dougie were also spending the night in a tent close to the hotel. They had come to the pub for some warmth and had brought along a pack of cards.

'Anyone for a game of gin rummy?' asked Dougie.

Steve took up the invitation but Dean passed, as did I. I wasn't much of a card player. Even though I wasn't in on the game, we all continued to chat anyway in the small confines of the walkers' bar.

Jimmy and Dougie – like Dean and Steve – were long-distance walking veterans. As someone who was new to it all, I asked them about the correct etiquette when you started chatting to a fellow walker but you were clearly marching at different paces and had different destinations.

'Aye,' said Dougie, dealing out the cards. 'Do you get there later or walk alone? Mind you, not everyone wants to chat. There's those that talk and those that don't.'

The congregation in the walkers' bar swelled further when an older gentleman came in, bought himself a dram and sat down next to me. He was Klaus from Germany and he was facing the prospect of having to get up at the crack of dawn to drive to Hull to catch a ferry to Rotterdam. Klaus sighed and took a sip of his whisky. This was the final night of his umpteenth trip to a country he had fallen madly in love with a long time ago.

'This here is where Scotland starts for me,' he said in a soft voice. 'Rannoch Moor and Glencoe.'

Klaus' favourite part of Scotland was the far northwest and he began reeling off the names of mountains he had climbed and climbed again. 'Suilven... Canisp... Stac Pollaidh... Cul Mor... Quinag...' It was like a poetry recital and his pronunciation of those exotic-sounding ancient Scottish hills was spot on.

After some more chat and one last beer, I decided it was time to hit the hay and rose from my spot to bid everyone goodnight. 'Is that you away to your wee posh room?' piped up Dougie from behind his hand of cards. 'Think of me out there tonight in my tent!'

— *Day Four*
  West Highland Way
  Inveroran to Kings House
  Ten miles

After a blissfully sound sleep – with apologies to Dougie in his tent – I was up bright and early for a magnificent cooked breakfast before returning to my room and lounging around for a bit. Eventually, I gathered my stuff together and sauntered downstairs to check out. I asked if anyone had left yet.

'They're all gone,' said Koa. 'You're the last one.'

'I am?' I gulped.

I didn't like the sound of being the last one.

I had pictured me setting off for Rannoch Moor around the same time as some other guests and being able to tag along with them. But I'd been much too complacent. There had been a few walking types at breakfast but I had done nothing more than wish them a good morning before tucking into my bacon and eggs.

Kurt, the young German from the bar last night, had clearly upped and left, while Dean and Steve, and Dougie and Jimmy, had been camping not far from the hotel. Perhaps I could track down their tents? If they hadn't already packed up and gone.

I cursed myself for not coming to some sort of arrangement last night to walk with any of them this morning. Because now I was faced with the wholly unappealing prospect of having to cross notoriously bleak and exposed Rannoch Moor on my own – and I didn't entirely trust myself not to completely freak out.

'Wh-what's the weather forecast?' I asked Koa, failing to mask my mounting panic.

'Just a second,' he replied, leaving his desk only to return a few moments later with a printout of an up-to-date weather report for the West Highlands.

I quickly scanned the page.

'Gales throughout the day… rain persistent… very difficult walking conditions where exposed…'

Christ almighty.

'Bet you wish you hadn't asked,' said Koa.

I was still staring in abject horror at the printout of bad tidings.

'Best of luck with it,' offered my host.

'Thanks,' I croaked.

Upon taking my first tentative steps outside, I was struck by how different everything looked from the previous evening. It was as if I was viewing the landscape through a filter that only served to make my surroundings appear more menacing. Perhaps it was my imagination, or more likely it was down to the overnight deterioration in the weather. The sky was filled with dark clouds and the rain was becoming more persistent by the second.

In an ungainly scramble, I pulled on my waterproof trousers for the first time and swapped my baseball cap for a woolly hat. I then raised the hood of my jacket and put on a pair of gloves – because there would be no shelter for the next ten miles. I peered up at the hill I'd scurried down last night to reach the hotel. My hope was that I might spot a walker or two heading towards me. I gave it a few minutes, waiting for the appearance of a bright bobble hat or a colourful jacket but no one was coming my way.

Turning my back on the empty hill, I set out along a lonely road, keeping an eye out for the tents of my friends from the walkers' bar last night, but there was no canvas in sight. It was just me, trudging towards Rannoch Moor in heavy rain. It then occurred to me that my only chance of company on the moor would be if I managed to catch up with someone. And so it was that, within a matter of seconds, I went from walking to speed-walking to jogging… to outright sprinting.

When the road came to an abrupt end, I negotiated a gate then resumed my running along a gradually rising stone path. To my right lay Loch Tulla and beyond it I could just make out a train travelling south. I pictured passengers sipping coffee in warm carriages while letting someone else deliver them to their destination.

Despite the rain, I stopped for a moment to look at the section of my map that I'd been staring at late last night in my room and again this morning after breakfast. The section that was relevant to me now was the one with the words 'Black Mount' written in big letters. I didn't like the sound of Black Mount… it sounded worse than Rannoch Moor. In fact, this map was beginning to resemble Tolkien's Middle Earth.

I scanned the sky for Ringwraiths riding winged beasts but couldn't see any, which was just as well. I wouldn't have stood a chance against the Dark Lord Sauron's servants because there was nowhere to hide in this barren place. I ran on hesitantly – if such a thing was possible – while trying to ignore the group of dark jagged mountains off to my left that I really didn't like the look of. Frankly, they were scaring me even though I wasn't required to go anywhere near them.

The rain – now torrential – was bouncing off my jacket

hood while the increasing wind was giving me a buffeting. Never had I felt so exposed. Conditions were woeful, I was becoming increasingly unnerved by the starkness of the terrain and I was doubting my ability to see this through. I tried telling myself that this was just another test along the Way and that I'd passed a few already. The truth was that I had done well so far on my own. But still…

I continued on the rocky road, hoping not to come a cropper, and my spirits rose when I thought I could make out a figure up ahead. But as I got closer and the person hadn't moved an inch, I realised it was a small bridge. I was still getting over that cruel disappointment when the landscape opened up completely and I found myself alone on Rannoch Moor.

To the east, as far as my panicked eyes could see, spread a gloomy wilderness of bogs, boulders and dark pools of water. This was like the Dead Marshes in The Lord of the Rings. I'd have Gollum to contend with any minute now. And to the west stood those menacing mountains which I still didn't care for. This place was desolate, inhospitable. Bleak. It had an undeniable otherworldly beauty but I didn't wish to linger. I would much rather escape such an alien scene than hang about admiring it.

The wind now sweeping across the moor was of sufficient strength to make me unsteady on my feet while the rain continued to soak and mock me. At least I had the right gear on. I peered ahead. The path was clear but it stretched too far into the distance for my liking.

Aware that I was cowering in these awful conditions, I decided to try to cut a more confident figure by striding on with some semblance of purpose. Not that anyone was watching me. But as I battled on, I saw through the driving rain something up ahead that was not part of this drab moor. Something that was bright orange in colour. I squinted and knew for sure that it was a backpack on the shoulders of another human being.

I was saved!

I transformed into the running man again as I raced to catch up – the rain and wind somewhat hampering my progress – and soon realised that there were two of them. The Walkers. My kind of people.

Before I drew level with them, I slowed to a walking pace so as not to startle them or appear crazed. And when I called 'hello' I tried to do so without sounding desperate. They said hello back from within the hoods of their cagoules. They were a youngish couple and it was difficult to have any sort of conversation in such atrocious conditions but I picked up that they were Johan and Sophie. And that they were from Belgium. Of course they were.

I blurted out something about it being good to see other people out here.

'You are not alone!' cried Johan.

'This is Rannoch Moor!' I shouted back, somewhat obviously.

'Pardon?!' yelled Johan.

My words appeared to have been lost in the wind, so I tried again.

'This is Rannoch Moor! This is the most exposed part!'

'Yes!' cried Johan. 'Exposed, definitely!'

Poor Johan. In addition to being battered by the elements, he was having to put up with my terrible chat.

I thought it best that I give him and Sophie a break from my inane wittering. They were on a special journey together and really didn't need some rambling, possibly deranged Scotsman latching on to them. Plus I realised that I didn't even have to play gooseberry. I could simply walk on ahead of them, though not too fast, safe in the knowledge that I had a pair of Belgians watching my back.

So I shouted to Johan and Sophie that I would be pressing on and thus marched on ahead while glancing back occasionally to check that they were still there. They didn't seem to be in much of a hurry. Either that or they were struggling. Whatever the case, I adjusted my pace accordingly, even though I wanted off this wretched moor as quickly as possible.

When I reached Ba Bridge – the River Ba rushing beneath it and flowing eastwards across the moor – I stopped to put on my fleece, which for some reason I hadn't been wearing. Call it an oversight, call it stupidity for thinking a jacket and a thin base-layer top would be sufficient on a day like this in a place like this.

Admittedly, my timing for trying to fix this clothing deficiency wasn't great. Standing at the most exposed section of the West Highland Way, I faced an almighty struggle, taking off my jacket and grasping onto it in high winds while trying to put on my fleece.

I had just finished fighting with said fleece and had somehow successfully pulled it over my head when Johan and Sophie caught up with me. They no doubt thought I was demented and, as if to drive home that fact, I cried out: 'Would you like me to take a picture of the two of you?'

Johan looked at Sophie.

Sophie looked at Johan.

'No, it's okay!' shouted Johan.

I'd thought that a photo of the two of them on Ba Bridge with the combined backdrop of moor and mountains would have made a nice memento of their time together on the West Highland Way. Couples were often in need of a passer-by to take a picture of them in memorable locations. Maybe just not now… when we were all being struck in the face by the horizontal rain and the ferocious wind was forcing us to stand at odd angles in an effort to remain upright. Johan and Sophie probably preferred to experience the wildness of Rannoch Moor without the need for a picture. Or possibly they thought that picture would be rubbish.

Once again, I thought it best that I leave them in peace and so, with my jacket back on over my fleece, I forged on ahead of my guardian Belgians for the second time.

At one point I stopped to look back across the moor and Johan and Sophie were mere specks – though reassuring ones – in the distance. Carrying on, I then saw the strangest sight up ahead, just off the path. A tent. A tiny yellow tent. Who in their right mind would think that pitching a tent in the middle of Rannoch Moor was a good idea? The tent was flapping madly in the wind and looked like it was about to take off. I wondered if anyone was inside and, if so, what the heck were they up to? Reading a good book? Thinking about what they might cook for tea? Having a quiet nap?

Still shaking my head at the incongruous sight of the tent, I trudged on. Soon the path began to descend and in the distance I could actually make out cars travelling on the A82. It wouldn't be long until I was off this flipping moor.

There was still time though for one final fright. Glancing up to a heather-clad hillock, I saw the dark head of an animal staring at me from behind a large rock. The odds were that it was a deer but I had decided that it was a panther and began legging it down the track towards the road. Now running beneath the imposing mass of Meall a'Bhuiridh, I could just make out the chairlifts of the Glencoe ski resort.

My moor adventure was behind me and I had been well and truly Rannoched. It had been something of an ordeal but now that it was over, I found myself laughing. Partly at my silliness but also because of the sheer thrill of the experience.

The section of the West Highland Way that I'd been dreading the most had turned out to be the most exhilarating. On some level, I had actually enjoyed it. And why not? I was a Scotsman wandering in the most Scottish of landscapes in the most awful Scottish weather. I should be okay with this... I was okay with this.

There was one more thrill to come before I reached the shelter of the remote Kings House Hotel and that was my first sight of Buachaille Etive Mor (the Big Herdsman of Etive), the massive pyramid-shaped mountain which guards the eastern entrance to Glencoe. And I'd thought Beinn Dorain was a sight to behold...

I then passed the whitewashed Blackrock cottage – as seen on many a Scottish postcard – and took great care in crossing the road before following the path down to the Kings House. The hotel looked the worse for wear but frankly I didn't care. Checking my watch, I was surprised to note that it was only half-past twelve. I had left the Inveroran Hotel at around ten. I had therefore covered ten miles, including Rannoch Moor, in two-and-a-half hours. Of course I had spent a good chunk of that time running to eventually catch up with a couple of Belgians and some of it sprinting away from what likely wasn't a panther.

I stumbled into the climbers' bar of the Kings House looking as if I had just been plucked from the North Sea. The first thing I did was remove my soaking-wet jacket and also my waterproof trousers (I had on other trousers beneath – I'm not one for sitting in a pub in my pants). I then sat down at a table with a heavy sigh. The only other customers in the climbers' bar were a couple having lunch, with a collie dog lying and dozing at their feet.

'It's wet out there,' said the man, looking up from his bowl of soup.

I nodded, still trying to catch my breath.

'Have you come far?' asked his wife, who was halfway through a plate of haggis, neeps and tatties.

'I've just crossed Rannoch Moor,' I replied, with a touch of pride.

'Well done you!' she said.

Deborah and Gordon were from London and their snoozing collie dog was Molly.

'Just getting my last taste of Scotland before we cross the border,' smiled Deborah, nodding at her dish of haggis.

Deborah was Scotland's biggest fan: 'I love it up here'. So much so that she had a high opinion of Scottish cuisine.

For the past fortnight, she and Gordon had been travelling around the Highlands in their campervan, as they did most years.

'The weather's been a bit mixed,' said Deborah, 'but that's to be expected.'

'We don't come to Scotland for the weather,' added Gordon.

Having finished his soup, he approached the bar to see if he could borrow a step ladder.

'No problem at all,' said the barman, who was back with one in a matter of minutes, passing it over the counter.

Gordon promptly marched outside with the step ladder under his arm. Deborah explained that the skylight on their campervan wasn't shutting properly. Gordon wanted to get up on the roof to try to fix it. I was next to approach the bar, ordering the soup of the day – cream of broccoli – and a coffee to help warm me up after my epic morning on Rannoch Moor.

I also mentioned to the barman my present dilemma, my Kings House conundrum so to speak. I explained that I had a room booked but that I was now swithering. It was, after all, only lunchtime and I was worried that I should maybe be carrying on to Kinlochleven, a distance of nine miles.

Staying put was by far the more attractive option, given the warmth of the Kings House and the dreadful conditions outside. But if I made an effort to carry on over the Devil's Staircase to Kinlochleven, it would make my final day on the West Highland Way less of a monstrous trek. Whereas remaining here for the rest of the day would leave me with a twenty-four mile yomp to reach Fort William. My question was: should I stick or twist?

'Let me check the forecast for tomorrow,' suggested the barman.

He came back and reported: 'Dry, basically. Meant to be really sunny, too.'

I looked out the window of the bar. It was still bucketing down. The Devil's Staircase held zero appeal just now. I was staying right where I was.

'Decision made?' asked Deborah.

'Definitely,' I said.

I then clocked the bottle of Glenfarclas 105 among the numerous whiskies on display. I was most certainly stopping here tonight if they were stocking my favourite dram. Heck, I'd walked seventy-two miles in the space of three-and-a-half days. Sure, I was leaving myself with a massive twenty-four miles to accomplish tomorrow but I'd worry about that later. I was taking the rest of the day off! It felt good and the steaming bowl of cream of broccoli soup, served with a big hunk of bread, made me feel even better. A happy Gordon came back into the bar with the step ladder, campervan skylight fixed. He then settled the meal bill, so that he and Deborah could continue their journey south with Molly the collie.

'Enjoy the rest of your walk – and the rest of the day off!' said Deborah.

'Will do,' I grinned. 'Safe journey.'

I leaned back in my seat, feeling properly warmed up now and completely relaxed.

The barman came over and handed me my room key and I was just about to retire to my quarters for an afternoon nap when the door of the climbers' bar swung open and in stumbled a soaked figure in a blue coat with a big orange backpack and an even bigger grin on his face.

'No way,' I said.

'Mind if I join you?' grinned Andy.

Well, the least I could do was buy the man a drink. I went and got a couple of pints while Andy climbed out of his waterproofs and sat down.

'How are your feet?' I asked upon my return with two celebratory glasses of ale.

'A bit better since I last saw you,' said Andy. 'My knee's still giving me grief but I'm coping.'

He had begun his day in Bridge of Orchy, climbing over the hill to Inveroran and crossing Rannoch Moor in atrocious conditions to get here, and still he was intent on tackling the Devil's Staircase.

'I don't fancy it in this weather,' said Andy, 'but I need to get to Kinlochleven tonight. Otherwise I'll never make it to Fort William tomorrow. What about you?'

I was almost embarrassed to tell him that I'd chosen to hole up here in the Kings House for the rest of the day and embark on an epic final leg of the West Highland Way come the morning.

'Is that daft?' I asked him.

'Ach, you'll be fine,' said Andy. 'You just need an early start.'

Our eyes then turned to the door of the climbers' bar as it swung open again to reveal two more weather-beaten souls.

'Bloody heck,' said a drenched Dean.

'Nice day for it,' commented a similarly saturated Steve.

The Derby duo were in the Kings House and once they'd shed their waterproofs and sat down, I introduced them to Andy. The four of us compared notes on crossing Rannoch Moor. I described my relief at managing to catch up with a couple from Belgium... and then Andy mentioned his chance encounter with a party of Belgian schoolchildren.

'Eh?' I said, quite understandably.

It turned out that a cold and wet Andy had at one point dived into the only clump of trees on Rannoch Moor in order to gain temporary protection from the wind and rain and to put on some extra clothing. While he was sorting himself out and enjoying his refuge, he heard someone shouting at him. Andy looked up to see a man calling to him from the path. The man wanted to know if the trees offered much in the way of shelter. Andy nodded and the man blew a whistle. The next Andy knew, dozens of shaken-looking children were piling into the tiny wooded area to join him. They were Belgian children and the man with the whistle was their school teacher.

He explained to Andy that each year he brought a group of pupils over to Scotland and had them walk the West Highland Way. 'Those kids must hate him,' I said.

'They didn't exactly look like they were having the time of their lives,' said Andy, who had left the Belgian school party in among the trees as he resumed his walk.

Dean then described how he and Steve had been walking past a thicket of trees on the otherwise barren moor when they had heard voices.

'I thought we were imagining it,' said Dean. 'But sure enough when we looked into the trees we saw a whole bunch of people.'

'The Belgians,' said Andy.

'I wonder if they're still there now?' I asked.

Just as we were all pondering the fate of the party of Belgian schoolchildren, Andy leapt up from his seat and pointed out the window. 'There they are!' he cried.

We all stared outside and saw perhaps fifteen youths, some of them in shorts, trudging through the rain on the far side of the river that ran behind the Kings House.

'That's not all of them,' said Andy.

'They must have lost a few...' said Steve.

'So they're carrying on over the Devil's Staircase in this weather?' marvelled Dean.

'Poor souls,' I said.

Talk then turned to the tiny yellow tent pitched on the middle of Rannoch Moor.

'Apparently it's some guy from Estonia – supposedly he's been there for days,' said Dean, who had heard this from some fellow walkers.

'What's he doing?' I asked.

'Camping, I suppose,' shrugged Steve.

At which point, three young women burst into the bar. Two of them, in sports gear complete with brightly coloured running shoes, grabbed on to the nearest chairs and started doing stretching exercises. The other woman sat down and explained that the energetic pair busy working out in the climbers' bar were sisters, running the West Highland Way together. Us chaps, sitting with our pints, were suitably gobsmacked and all of a sudden felt like a right bunch of slackers.

Although Ailsa, who was chatting to us, had taken a seat, having forgone any kind of stretching routine, she turned out to be no slouch herself. After setting off from Tyndrum first thing, she had bumped into the running sisters near Bridge of Orchy and had kept pace with them across Rannoch Moor to arrive here at the Kings House. This meant that Ailsa had done something like twenty miles by lunchtime, which was twice what I had managed. I was having a hard time getting my head round all this excessive mileage.

A soaked bloke in full waterproofs then strode into the Kings House. I recognised the face inside the jacket hood. It was Dougie from the Inveroran Hotel last night. He nodded and made straight for the bar where he obtained two Mars bars then turned and said 'can't stop' and marched out, gripping a chocolate bar in each hand. He was a man on a mission… my new hero.

Once the running sisters, who were from Edinburgh, had done enough stretching and grabbed a quick bite to eat, they were ready to climb over – or more likely sprint over – the Devil's Staircase. We all wished them luck and waved goodbye. No doubt they'd be in Fort William by teatime.

After a second pint – as per the rules – Andy rose from his seat. 'I'd better get going,' he sighed.

It was nearing three o'clock and he was no closer to Kinlochleven. 'I'll see you out,' I said, as if this was my own home. I was getting quite comfortable in the Kings House.

I waved Andy off in the rain as he crossed the bridge over the river and marched off in the direction of the Devil's Staircase. He was walking much more freely than when I'd first bumped into him near Tyndrum. Hopefully, I would see him at the finish line. We had exchanged phone numbers with the intention of meeting up for a celebratory pint in Fort William later on tomorrow before Andy caught an evening train back to Glasgow. I would then have the Great Glen Way to deal with but I'd worry about that later...

After the luxury of an afternoon nap in my spartan but more than adequate single room, I joined Dean and Steve for dinner in the climbers' bar. The warren-like Kings House had a lounge too but Dean and Steve, who had stayed here several times before on previous West Highland Way adventures, insisted upon eating in the climbers' bar.

'It's tradition,' explained Steve. I was happy to participate in their tradition.

The pair of them ordered venison burgers while I couldn't see past the haggis, neeps and tatties after watching Deborah polish off a plate of it at lunchtime.

'Food tastes better up here,' said Steve between bites of his burger. 'If you had this in Derby, it wouldn't taste the same.'

As we sat chatting, I received a text from Andy. He was safe and dry in Kinlochleven but had endured a torrid time on the Devil's Staircase due to all the rain.

'The Devil's Staircase is now the Devil's Waterslide!' reported Andy. Seemingly a stream on the hill had become more of a gushing river. 'Knee deep in water!' said Andy. Thank goodness he was safe.

Hopefully, it would have all calmed down by the time I tackled the Devil's Staircase tomorrow in dry weather.

I went and double-checked the forecast with the barman.

'Well, the skiers are here,' he said.

'Skiers?' I gulped. 'Does that mean it's going to snow?'

'No, no,' smiled the barman. 'Quite the opposite

actually.' Skiers turning up in numbers at the Kings House was a good thing. That meant the weather was going to be clear so that they could fully enjoy the slopes of Glencoe.

'It's definitely going to be dry tomorrow,' the barman assured me.

Feeling relaxed, I ordered a Glenfarclas 105 nightcap then toddled off back to my room for a good night's sleep before the final leg of the West Highland Way to Fort William, Devil's Staircase and all.

In the hotel corridor, I bumped into a Belgian. Naturally. Joost was a bit tipsy and chatty. He was a big music fan. Since he was from Belgium, I mentioned dEUS, by far my favourite Belgian band (and indeed the only Belgian band I knew). Joost just happened to be a big dEUS fan too. Maybe everyone in Belgium was. My bedtime was delayed somewhat as Joost and I ran through dEUS' extensive back catalogue and compared gigs we'd been to (him Antwerp, me Glasgow).

Back in my room some time later, I speculated as to whether a walking holiday in Belgium would involve me bumping into loads of Scottish people.

— *Day Five*
  West Highland Way
  Kings House to Fort William
  Twenty-four miles

With a massive twenty-four miles ahead of me, including the small matter of the Devil's Staircase, I was up with the lark for a fortifying breakfast of smoked haddock and poached egg. I also went heavy on the toast, given what lay ahead of me. The only other super-early riser seated in the Kings House dining room tackling the most important meal of the day was Ailsa from the climbers' bar the previous afternoon. She was having to be on the move sharp because she was booked on a teatime train from Fort William to Edinburgh. Mind you, given the astonishing amount of ground she had managed to cover in such a short space of time yesterday, she was probably on course to complete the West Highland Way by lunchtime.

Ailsa asked if I fancied setting off with her on the final leg of the journey. I wasn't sure I could cope, imagining that she would leave me in the dust, but I agreed to join her. I was glad of the company and I think she was too... I just had to try to keep up.

We were on the march by eight, both of us cheered by the sight of several deer near the hotel, the clear blue sky and the inspiring mountain scenery. I was also buoyed by Ailsa's presence. I don't think I'd ever met such a relentlessly positive person. She was unbelievably cheery and chatted away happily. Ailsa, who was in her twenties, lived in Edinburgh although she had spent her childhood in the Highlands. Having the Cairngorms on her doorstep had ensured an early love of the outdoors. Clearly someone who liked to challenge herself, Ailsa enjoyed snowboarding and sailing and had even walked the Camino de Santiago in Spain. She spoke of the camaraderie she had experienced on that iconic journey and the inspiring stories of fellow pilgrims. There was surely a little of that spirit too on the West Highland Way.

Our brisk early pace was mostly down to my youthful companion. I was just making sure that I didn't lag behind as we strode westwards beneath Beinn a'Chrulaiste towards the head of Glencoe, with Buachaille Etive Mor still hogging the limelight, despite some hefty competition.

Having made swift progress, we quickly found ourselves at the foot of the Devil's Staircase.

'It doesn't look too bad,' I said, gazing at the path that zigzagged up the hill to the highest point of the West Highland Way. It looked a fair climb but it wasn't quite the diabolical challenge that I'd built up in my mind.

'It shouldn't take us long,' smiled Ailsa. 'Especially in this lovely weather.'

I tried to imagine Andy tackling this towering obstacle in torrential rain yesterday. It would have been a markedly different experience.

The Devil's Staircase was constructed in the eighteenth century as part of the road-building programme of General Wade. It took four hundred soldiers to complete a path whose ominous name was coined by those charged with the arduous task of building it in often atrocious conditions. The snaking nature of the track ensured a gradual ascent as Ailsa and I made for the top of the staircase. As we gained altitude, the view back to the imposing mountains of Glencoe became ever more incredible – and it was this that landed me in trouble.

Approximately two thirds of the way up the Devil's Staircase, I turned around once more to take in the dramatic vista and my legs turned to jelly. I couldn't move. And I couldn't look. I took my eyes off the peaks and stared down at the ground at my feet.

My head was spinning – the dizziness was debilitating – and the thing I wanted more than anything in the world was to not be on this hill. I wanted down but I couldn't do anything about it. I called ahead to Ailsa to inform her that I was in trouble.

'What's the matter?' she asked.

I muttered something about the height getting to me

and my legs not working. 'Let's talk about something else,' she suggested.

'Um,' was about all I could manage in response. So Ailsa did most of the talking. She began by telling me some of her favourite countries and by the time she had moved on to her favourite foods, I was on the move again. Much more slowly and more hesitantly than before – with my legs not fully co-operating – but moving nonetheless. I still wouldn't take my eyes off the ground and when Ailsa asked me what my favourite film was, I couldn't think of one despite being a film fanatic. Eventually I mumbled something about The Third Man.

Seeing that I was still struggling, Ailsa described how she had been at her lowest ebb yesterday morning in miserable conditions near Bridge of Orchy when the two sisters from Edinburgh had caught up with her and encouraged her to run with them for a bit. With her spirits lifted by such effervescent company, she had got all the way across Rannoch Moor before bursting in the door of the Kings House.

And now Ailsa was aiding me. This was the spirit of the Way. Her vitality and optimism were having a positive effect, helping me through my most difficult spell. Whenever I so much as mentioned my trouble with heights, Ailsa interrupted me and told me not to talk about it. It wasn't a topic up for discussion.

We moved on to favourite music as we neared the top of the Devil's Staircase. I realised that my eyes weren't glued to the ground anymore and that I could actually look up without freaking out. That was until all I could see beyond the crest of the hill was sky as I became convinced that I was approaching a sheer drop and that I was about to fall off the back of the Devil's Staircase. And so my legs failed me again. Standing rooted to the spot, I explained my concern to Ailsa whose response was to bound on ahead and report back that there was nothing to worry about. All that was waiting for me was the path winding down the other side. My invaluable (and incredibly patient) walking companion came back and walked me to the top. Although I made sure that I stuck to the left edge of the path as it swung left, just to make absolutely sure that I didn't fall off. Even though there was nowhere to fall. If I had strayed from the path and tripped, the worst that could have happened was that I rolled gently in the heather. I really was a shambles.

On the summit of the Devil's Staircase, the two of us sat down next to a cairn. Ailsa didn't even ask if I was okay. Possibly because that would only be drawing attention to the problem. Anyway, I'd made it. Thanks to her.

Gazing north across the Leven valley to the Mamores mountains and beyond them Ben Nevis – Britain's highest mountain being quite the visual marker for the finish line in Fort William – it was clear that we still had some way to go. At least the view forward wasn't as bad as the one back. Both were breathtaking but this one was easier for me to cope with. The Mamores were further away and not in my face like Glencoe, and I could see the winding path dropping gradually towards Kinlochleven.

Ailsa and I stood up and began the long descent on a stony track. Crossing a small stream, I thought again of Andy and how it must have been a completely different picture for him yesterday in the incessant rain. He'd said in his text that he had been 'knee deep' in water. I tried to imagine the scene and shuddered at the thought.

After powering through the next couple of miles with the sun shining down on us, Ailsa and I paused for some much-needed refreshments. I was going to make do with plain water but was offered some tea. I'm not a tea drinker but accepted and Ailsa poured me a cup from her flask. It was black tea but in the circumstances, with the surrounding forest and mountain scenery, and the Devil's Staircase behind me, it was a candidate for the best hot drink I'd ever had. I made sure to savour every sip.

On we marched along the undulating path until it began to drop sharply and we had our first glimpse of Kinlochleven. When we finally reached the village, Ailsa sat down on a bench while I nipped to the nearest shop for a sandwich and more water. When I returned, I sat down on a separate bench from Ailsa and changed my socks, explaining to her the ten-mile rule and how it had served me well on what had been a blister-free journey so far.

Three hours had passed since our departure from the Kings House. Thanks to our early start, it was only eleven o'clock. Ailsa's train was at half-past five and we had fourteen miles to go. I figured that we were in a strong position to make it to Fort William with some time to spare. This was the new me. I had become a lean, mean walking machine and would need to remain one for at least another week if I was also going to accomplish the Great Glen Way and Speyside Way.

Leaving Kinlochleven required a significant amount of effort as Ailsa and I faced a seriously steep climb through woodland. The compensation for our hard legwork came in the form of commanding views over Loch Leven. The path eventually levelled out as we connected with an old military road and headed westwards through the mountain pass of Lairigmor. This proved to be another absolute highlight of the West Highland Way, wandering down the long, wide glen in the sunshine, with the sharp peak of Stob Ban – one of the alluring Mamores – drawing our gazes.

Ailsa then suggested that we run for a bit. 'To that building there,' she said, pointing down the glen to an isolated ruined croft. She promptly set off at speed along the stony track and I did my best to keep up with her. I had to admit it was fun, picking up the pace in such epic surroundings. At the outset of my journey, I could never have imagined me flying down a glen with a backpack.

I had raced across Rannoch Moor but that was me desperately trying to catch up with someone and, ahem, running away from a possible panther. This was infinitely more enjoyable and the fact that we weren't far now from Fort William added to the thrill.

When I caught up with Ailsa at the abandoned croft, she congratulated me. She wasn't being sarcastic either; she genuinely meant it. We had come a long way (Devil's Staircase and all) and were now bearing down on that finish line. I felt more energised than at any previous point in the journey. I was full of adrenalin, a big achievement within reach. The sun was shining and Scotland looked its best.

We pressed on as the Way took a sharp turn north to lead us past a tree plantation before we began the gradual descent into Glen Nevis. The mighty form of Ben Nevis, with its snowy summit and deep-cut gullies, towered ahead of us, doing a grand job of being the biggest mountain in the land.

Some people, upon completing the West Highland Way, climbed Ben Nevis as a grand finale but there was no danger of me doing such a thing. Ailsa, who naturally had scaled Ben Nevis before, reckoned I'd manage it no problem. I duly reminded her of my recent panic on the comparatively small matter of the Devil's Staircase. But Miss Positivity insisted that if I put my mind to it, I could easily conquer Ben Nevis. I stared at it but couldn't see it happening.

Walk This Way

The mountain I was never going to climb temporarily disappeared from view as we trekked down through a forest, crossing a couple of streams and enjoying the cooler air. There was another outbreak of running – instigated by Ailsa, not me – and then we reached a clearing where the track rose sharply one last time before winding down towards Fort William. All the while, I kept gawping – and gulping – at Ben Nevis. You really couldn't miss it.

Ailsa and I parted company on a pavement on the edge of town, saying our goodbyes as cars sped past. She was off to the finish line in the town centre and then the station to catch her train. Whereas I was taking a slight detour before completing the Way.

Andy had not long texted me to say that he was in the Ben Nevis pub. I had done a quick map search on my phone and found that said pub was at the foot of the main path up Ben Nevis. And now I wasn't far from it at all. I had suggested to Ailsa that she join us but she hadn't as much time to play with as I had. So I ended up swinging by the place on my own. I ordered a pint then had a look around but Andy was nowhere to be seen. He wasn't in the bar and neither was he sitting in the lovely beer garden. So I sent him a text, asking where he was. He texted back, saying he was in the Ben Nevis pub and asking if I was nearly there yet. Confused, I thought I'd better call him.

We quickly established that I was in the wrong pub. It turned out that there were two Ben Nevises (well, three including the mountain) and Andy was sitting in the one on Fort William's High Street next to the finish point of the West Highland Way. What a mess I'd made of this... I sat down in the beer garden anyway and sank my pint beneath Ben Nevis, having walked from the outskirts of Scotland's largest city to the foot of the nation's highest mountain.

Over the course of five unforgettable days, I had wrestled with Loch Lomond's infernal eastern shore and survived the Ledge of Doom. I'd crossed a dung-filled quagmire and got cross with Crianlarich. I'd run across Rannoch Moor and conquered the Devil's Staircase (after a major wobble). Plus I had met some feral goats and countless Belgians. And now it was time to make a second attempt to meet Andy. And actually complete the West Highland Way.

I traipsed down a quiet lane to the town centre and walked the length of Fort William's pedestrianised High Street until I came to Gordon Square where the bronze sculpture of a walker sitting on a bench signified journey's end. I'd felt a greater sense of achievement sitting back there in that beer garden beneath Ben Nevis. I didn't linger in the square as I was kind of getting in the way of a bunch of kids, who were busy circling the sculpture on BMXs.

As soon as I walked into the correct Ben Nevis pub, Andy rose from his seat to shake my hand as we congratulated each other on our walking accomplishments. 'Check this out,' said Andy, pulling out his phone to show me some footage of the Devil's Staircase from the previous day. Even on a five-inch screen the gushing water on the hill looked pretty scary.

Andy explained how later on, once safe and dry in Kinlochleven, he'd encountered the running sisters from Edinburgh again and learned how they had received a helping hand on the Devil's Staircase. They had been struggling to cross the swollen stream when a walker further down the hill had seen that they were in trouble and had raced back up to assist them. He had reached out for their bags and helped the two of them across the water. The person who had come to their aid was none other than Dougie, who had just risen even further in my estimation.

'Fancy a pint?' asked Andy, who had the air of a man basking in his achievement and free of any further blister agony. I wasn't about to say no.

After a beer we shifted to the Grog & Gruel pub across the road where I spotted a bottle of Glenfarclas 105 on the shelf. Andy opted for a Jura as he joined me in a celebratory dram to toast our successes.

It was the end of the road for him. While I still had many more miles to go...

On my way: Treading towards Dumgoyne early on the first morning

A bonnie, bonnie scene: By the banks of Loch Lomond before it all got rather tricky

Wild at heart: Day three on the West Highland Way and the scenery is really starting to sing

Feeding station: Unexpected trekking treats, including Granny's special recipe traditional Scottish tablet

The moor the merrier? Just happy to be leaving desolate Rannoch Moor behind me

Highway to hell: Having a diabolical time on the Devil's Staircase

Lock this way: Part two of my epic journey underway as I head towards the Highland capital

Walk this waterway: Clomping along next to the Caledonian Canal

The rolling stones: Worrying potential for falling boulders on the disused railway line alongside Loch Oich

Pine-cone panic: Hello? Is it me you're looking for? Quit playing games, Lionel

Don't play misty for me: Petrified in the forest as it all turns a bit Brothers Grimm

Monster view: Looking down on magnificent Loch Ness once the mist has cleared

Walk the line: Blithely ignoring the clear warning from the rail authorities at Cromdale station

Chain reaction: Ach no, not another one of these confounded gates

Field trip: Stepping stones across the Speyside countryside

Pinnacle of pubs: the legendary Fiddichside Inn in Craigellachie

GREAT
GLEN
WAY

The morning after the West Highland Way. No hangover (despite those celebratory drinks with Andy) and surprisingly few complaints from my legs, even though I had half-run that last part to Fort William in the company of athletic Ailsa.

I was in much better shape for the Great Glen Way than I had any right to expect. Sure, a day off would have been nice, a chance to recuperate before embarking on my second walking challenge. But this wasn't possible thanks to the genius planner who had decided he didn't need any rest days on his trek across Scotland.

What I definitely didn't need was another cooked breakfast. Instead I made do with a bowl of cereal and a slice of toast, washed down with orange juice and coffee. After checking out of my budget hotel in the centre of town, I headed straight to the supermarket across the road and picked up some bananas, oatcakes and water. When I emerged from the supermarket, it was bucketing down with rain. I responded by climbing into my waterproof trousers, while shoppers walked by pushing trolleys.

My first challenge regarding the Great Glen Way was finding the damn thing. After twice going the wrong way at a roundabout, I discovered the path behind a McDonald's, a blue thistle marker post indicating that I was on the right track. Hood up and shoulders hunched, I trudged along past an empty shinty pitch. A woman out walking her dog commented on the lousy weather. 'Maybe it'll clear up,' she said, not sounding too hopeful. I crossed a bridge over the River Lochy then found myself skirting the edge of a housing estate, with a grand view down Loch Linnhe. A short while later, I reached the towpath of the Caledonian Canal.

A good chunk of my next four days would be spent by the canal, which runs between Fort William and Inverness, cutting through the Great Glen and linking three lochs: Loch Lochy, Loch Oich and Loch Ness. The Caledonian Canal was designed and engineered by Thomas Telford and took almost two decades to construct. Opened in 1822, it created a through route from west coast to east coast.

I soon arrived at the Caledonian Canal's most famous feature, Neptune's Staircase, which mercifully was nothing like the Devil's Staircase. A photogenic flight of eight locks for raising or lowering boats, Neptune's Staircase is one of Fort William's foremost tourist attractions and there were a few people around in colourful cagoules, taking pictures in the rain. According to my Great Glen Way map, Neptune's Staircase was the only 'ascent' between Fort William and Gairlochy. If that was the case then I was in for a relatively easy day, especially with it only being eleven miles to Gairlochy.

The modest mileage was sensible planning – evidence of some method in my madness. I may not have granted myself the luxury of a day off after completing the West Highland Way but I would at least be able to enjoy a leisurely first day on the Great Glen Way, consisting of flat terrain over a relatively short distance.

Mind you, I had just come to a halt. Next to Neptune's Staircase was a rather nice-looking cafe. As I wasn't in much of a hurry, there was no harm in me popping in for a coffee. I took a seat by the window and stared out at the locks and the lashing rain. 'It's getting heavier,' a woman at the next table remarked to her friend.

I eked out my coffee for as long as I could before I slung my bag over my shoulders again and swapped the comfort of the cafe for the downpour outside. Continuing along the canal side, I passed a couple of moored barges. The towpath itself wasn't exactly teeming with traffic. Just the occasional jogger or dog-walker, with no sign of anyone else doing the Great Glen Way.

Despite that coffee in the cafe, I was feeling fairly lethargic but then I had just walked the West Highland Way. Plodding on, I stared at the raindrops splashing on the surface of the canal and then shifted my gaze to the flat, straight towpath stretching into the distance. After a while, I tuned out of that repetitive view and it took the noise of motorbikes – two youths spinning about in a nearby field – to snap me out of my dwam before I sleepwalked into the canal.

On I stumbled, with the racket of the motorbikes being replaced by the bleating of sheep. There was some mild excitement when a line of cyclists whizzed by heading south... and then it was just me again in the unceasing rain with only the canal for company and low-lying hills in the distance. The Great Glen Way wasn't so great so far. There was a distinct lack of drama. Maybe it was like the West Highland Way in that the excitement gradually increased? I was missing some of the adrenalin of the past couple of days. Oh, to be freaking out on the Great Glen equivalent of the Devil's Staircase, or Rannoch Moor...

On a map of Scotland, it looks as if someone has taken a ruler and drawn a straight line between Fort William and Inverness to create the Great Glen, which runs along an ancient fault line. I didn't mean to be finding fault with the

Great Glen Way experience. It was just that I didn't really feel as if I was walking in a glen right now. I'd clearly been spoiled by the surfeit of epic mountain scenery on the West Highland Way.

When I later drew level with a swing bridge on the canal, I checked my map and saw that I was barely two miles from Gairlochy. And it wasn't even lunchtime yet. Just when I had shaken off my tiredness and was feeling more fleetfooted on the flat towpath, my 'day' was drawing to an end. By the time I reached the canal locks at Gairlochy, the rain had stopped and the clouds were clearing to allow the sun to make a welcome appearance.

Gairlochy wasn't so much a village as a scattering of houses but it wasn't my base for the night. I was actually going to be spending the night in Spean Bridge, which was four miles east of where I stood and therefore some way off the official route. However, the B&B I had booked offered a complimentary pick-up service for walkers, so I gave them a call. Peter answered and said he was due to collect some guests at Gairlochy in an hour's time. I didn't want him to have to drive here twice but neither did I fancy hanging around for an hour…

It was only four miles and the sun was now shining, plus I really felt like I hadn't walked far enough – this was how much of a Walker I'd become – so I told Peter that I would happily walk to Spean Bridge.

'Are you sure?' he asked.

'Absolutely,' I replied. 'It's a fine day for it.'

So, after a change of socks, I set off along the road to Spean Bridge. I had only gone a couple of hundred yards when I bumped into a man out for a walk. He wasn't local though. He was John from Manchester, who was wild camping in the area with his wife. I told him I was doing the Great Glen Way but was now walking to Spean Bridge and would probably be looking for a pint upon my arrival.

'Top man,' smiled John, who had done a lot of walking in the Peak District and had also traipsed the length of the Pennine Way. This was his first time in Scotland and he and his wife were loving it. John reckoned people were drawn to the Highlands for the solitude as much as the scenery.

'You can be sharing the Pennine Way with hundreds of people,' he said, before turning and pointing south. 'I mean, look at that!' he exclaimed, indicating a series of snow-topped peaks, including Ben Nevis, lined up in the distance beneath a clear blue sky. 'Magic.'

It was a sight to behold and I was as delighted as John to be standing here witnessing it. I'd spent much of yesterday looking at Ben Nevis from the other side. John asked how many days I'd been walking and I explained that although this was my first day on the Great Glen Way, it was my sixth day overall, having just completed the West Highland Way.

'Fair play to you,' said John. 'At least you're in the glen now... not so hilly!'

Maybe I'd been wrong to complain about the shortage of drama on the Great Glen Way thus far. Who knew what the coming days would hold, on the long trek north to Inverness? There was Loch Ness to look forward to... and Loch Lochy!

I said cheerio to John and continued with what turned out to be a stunning walk to Spean Bridge amid beautiful countryside and with a near-constant view of Ben Nevis. These extra unexpected miles, which had nothing to do with the Great Glen Way, were easily outshining my entire morning by the canal.

After a blissful – and still blister-free – couple of miles, I came to a road junction and a car park busy with tourist buses. The tourists were taking pictures of the Commando Memorial, a striking bronze sculpture of three soldiers facing in the direction of Ben Nevis. Thousands of Commandos trained in the Spean Bridge area during the Second World War and the iconic monument commemorates those who lost their lives fighting for their country. I paused for a few moments among the crowds to observe the statue then crossed the car park and found the pavement that would take me down into Spean Bridge.

As I approached the village, I passed a roadside advertisement for the Highland Haggis Festival, which was to be held in Spean Bridge in a couple of weeks' time. I wondered how many different events could spring from Scotland's national dish? I once witnessed the World Haggis Eating Championships – at a Highland Games in Perthshire – and it was carnage. A bunch of hungry men scoffing haggis against the clock... a truly offal spectacle (sorry). Perhaps the Highland Haggis Festival also included a haggis speed-eating contest? Maybe haggis-throwing featured too? There might be… guess the weight of the haggis… find the haggis… and there was bound to be a prize for best-tasting haggis. All of a sudden, I felt quite hungry.

Crossing a high bridge over the River Spean, I arrived in Spean Bridge and found a cosy pub-restaurant within a former railway station building. I ordered a pint of Old Commando ale and took a seat by the window, with a nice view of the train platform. The Old Station was filled with young women and the barmaid explained that the local ladies' shinty team had just beaten Glasgow University, who were top of the league. Having taken a prize scalp, the local heroes were tucking into pizza and chips.

Now I was really hungry.

'Fancy some pizza?' the chef called to me from the kitchen area.

'Eh, sure, thanks,' I replied. I was ravenous. Over he came, with a couple of slices on a plate.

'You want chips?' he asked.

'Sure, that'd be great.'

He returned with a tray of chips, shovelling a pile of them on top of my pizza. Having just been given a surprise free meal, I felt obliged to come back here in the evening for my dinner.

'Would you like to make a booking for tonight?' asked the barmaid, reading my mind. 'We're usually quite busy.'

'Sure,' I answered. 'Is seven o'clock alright? It's just for one.'

'It's okay, we'll find you a woman!' piped up the chef.

I laughed and then got stuck into my pizza and chips. Having wolfed down my complimentary lunch, I continued to sip my pint of Old Commando while gazing out at the railway platform. Heaven right now was the Old Station in Spean Bridge.

A few hours later – after settling in at my nearby B&B and having a wee lie down – I was back again, tackling a bumper portion of the chef's fish and chips... along with another pint of Old Commando because it would have been rude not to. After I'd cleaned my plate and drained my glass, I sauntered back up the road to the B&B as a car sped past with the windows down and The Boys of Summer blaring into the night sky.

— Day Seven
  Great Glen Way
  Gairlochy to Fort Augustus
  Twenty-three miles

Breakfast in Spean Bridge was a delicious serving of smoked salmon and scrambled eggs with oatcakes. Afterwards, our genial host Peter drove me and a few other guests of Distant Hills B&B back to Gairlochy, so that we could reconnect with the Great Glen Way.

Rain battered the windscreen throughout the short journey and Peter, who had checked the local forecast, confirmed that it was supposed to chuck it down all day. He dropped us off by the canal and wished everyone all the best as we got ready to resume our respective journeys.

Crossing Gairlochy's swing bridge then initially following a gravel path through woods, I walked for a bit with Pippa and Kristal, two Zimbabwean ladies enjoying a Scottish walking holiday, even in this dire weather. For them, an abundance of great scenery made up for the distinct lack of sunshine.

Wildlife became a topic of conversation as I described my encounter with feral goats near the shores of Loch Lomond. I made no mention of previous panther sightings in Scotland but did confess to a long-held fear of cows as a result of the trauma of having been chased by one in my youth. Pippa laughed and began to recount a nerve-racking encounter with animals while walking in the wilds of Zimbabwe. I was expecting a terrifying tale of lions or elephants perhaps. However, poor Pippa had become unnerved when faced with a large flock of sheep. She had reached for her phone and called her mum whose blunt response was to tell her daughter to 'man up' since the very idea of being trampled by sheep – as opposed to, say, buffalo – was laughable. Although it didn't sound such a far-fetched notion to me, given my near-catastrophic cow episode. Trust nothing on four legs was my motto (I included cats in that but was totally fine with tables).

Pippa and Kristal's target for the day was Laggan Locks, whereas I was having to reach Fort Augustus. Much as I was enjoying chatting to them, I had double the number of miles on my agenda. After wishing them well for the rest of their Highland adventure, I picked up the pace and struck out on my own.

Following a sharp descent through woodland, I reached the shores of Loch Lochy. And wondered if perhaps the River Rivery flowed into this imaginatively named loch. Not only is Loch Lochy Scotland's third-deepest loch, it even boasts its own monster in the shape of Lizzie, a three-humped phenomenon, who is presumably a close cousin of the more internationally renowned Nessie. Striding along near the water's edge, I kept an eye out for any humps breaking the surface of the loch. In addition to offering the thrill of a possible monster sighting, what was great about Loch Lochy was that it was nothing like Loch Lomond with its accursed boulders and wretched tree roots. Mind you, I could have done with better weather for this undemanding loch-side stroll because the rain was getting ridiculous.

After a while, the path climbed away from the loch and I briefly found myself on a country road before crossing a bridge over the River Arkaig and ending up close to the loch shore again on a forest track. Passing a towering pile of tree trunks, I noted the warning sign: 'Do not climb on timber stacks – Danger'. I wasn't in the least tempted to start climbing on them. Even if Gary Sutherland and the Treacherous Stacks of Timber sounded like a potential sequel to Gary Sutherland and the Ledge of Doom.

Strolling along the gently undulating path, while enjoying regular views of Loch Lochy, it occurred to me that Ailsa would probably have jogged this section. After initially dismissing the idea, I was off! Not quite at breakneck speed but zippy enough for my seventh day on the road. My former running partner would have been proud of me. Though soon enough I slowed to speed-walking level, bent forward against a strengthening wind and the incessant rain. Then, when faced with a bit of an uphill, I was back to my normal walking pace.

A couple of grand houses stood among the trees on the opposite shore and I wondered if one of them was Letterfinlay Lodge. It was marked on my map for some reason and I was unsure whether I had passed it already or not. In fact, I would have appreciated a giant flag with a letter 'L' flying proudly from the roof of Letterfinlay Lodge because at least then I'd have known where I stood.

A cold breeze continued to sweep down the loch and I was beginning to feel numb with the constant wind and rain. This weather really was the pits. Conditions had been dreadful crossing Rannoch Moor but I was holed up in the Kings House by lunchtime. Whereas I wasn't expecting to reach Fort Augustus until early evening. The numbness did not even mask the pain in my ankles and shoulders. I was in sore need of a rest but it was too early in the day, with so many miles yet to be covered. In any case, there was nowhere to sit down. Everything was soaking wet anyway. My only option really was to keep going...

I trudged on, barely aware of my surroundings while blanking out the physical effort involved. Perhaps I could continue in this manner all the way to Inverness? It took an army of flying insects hitting me in the face to bring me back to my senses, as I tried to block the blighters off – unsuccessfully – with my hands.

I staggered past a ruined bothy (it was in a similar state to me) then finally reached the end of the forest track before crossing a bridge as well as a cattle grid to follow the road downhill towards Laggan Locks. I looked at my watch and saw that it was half-past twelve. It had taken me the best part of three hours to walk the length of Loch Lochy. Although it hadn't been anything like the ordeal that was Loch Lomond, I was still glad to have reached the end of it.

Next up was another stint alongside the Caledonian Canal but first I was hoping to find some temporary shelter from the wind and rain in tiny Laggan Locks. My eyes lit up when I clocked a barge that appeared to double as a pub. I had no hesitation in boarding The Eagle and ducked inside. Descending the steps to what indeed was a proper pub magically contained within the confines of a barge, I momentarily hesitated due to my drenched and muddy state.

'Don't worry about your shoes,' smiled the barmaid. 'Come on in and get yourself warmed up!'

She duly directed me to the bow of The Eagle where there was a handy drying room.

I hung up my dripping jacket and waterproof trousers – while keeping on my walking trousers, naturally – and returned to the bar for a bowl of tomato soup and a coffee.

Even after that winning combination, I still wasn't properly warmed up and so my thoughts turned to the possibility of a stiff whisky. Spotting the bottle of Glenfarclas on the shelf sealed the deal. My favourite malt was like a reviving rocket as I went from feeling pretty feeble to utterly invincible within a mere matter of seconds.

Ready to take on the world again – or at least the Caledonian Canal in the rain – I returned to the drying room and grabbed my jacket and waterproof trousers. I was delighted to find that both items were now bone dry, although I was just about to get soaked all over again. After clambering into my all-weather gear, I wandered back through to the bar, saying cheerio to the barmaid and to the family of cyclists who, within the past quarter-of-an-hour, had found refuge within the bowels of the barge.

Back on the canal towpath, I marched ahead purposefully, not caring a jot about the rain battering down on me. My carefree attitude may have had something to do with that cheeky Speyside number I'd just quaffed. But I soon realised that something wasn't quite right. The problem seemed to be my waterproof trousers... they didn't really fit anymore. Tight in the leg and also too short, they appeared to have significantly reduced in size. They couldn't possibly have shrunk that much during their short time in the drying room, could they? I also noted that my waterproof trousers looked a good deal muddier than before. I stopped and checked the label inside the waistband.

These weren't my trousers.

Although black like mine, they were a different brand. My trousers were back in the barge. I must have reached for the wrong pair in the drying room when getting ready to set off again. In doing so, I had inadvertently caused major trouser confusion. My embarrassment was complete upon my return to The Eagle as I descended the steps once more to explain why I was back.

'They must be my trousers,' said the mother of the cycling family as her husband and two children burst out laughing.

'I promise to get out of them right away,' I said, shaking my head and trying to make the best of a mortifying situation.

Back I went to the drying room, removing and hanging up the poor woman's trousers then grabbing hold of my own breeks – as I should have managed first time round. What a daft mistake to make. Mind you, it was probably just as well that I'd realised my ridiculous error when I did. Otherwise I might have had the woman pedalling after me in a pair of oversized waterproof trousers, hoping to do a vital swap in the great outdoors.

'All sorted!' I announced, emerging from the drying room in the correct trousers.

'That's good,' said the woman.

'You are wearing the right jacket, aren't you?' piped up her husband.

'Yep, pretty sure!' I replied. I was glad to have given them some amusement – and to be reunited with my breeks.

I headed off once again along the canal path, my movement no longer restricted by the tightness of someone else's trousers. A boat sailed by as the rain began to ease a little and soon I was swapping the towpath for a track through lovely pinewoods. Between the pleasant surroundings, the slight improvement in the weather, a recent change of socks whilst sitting in The Eagle and not least that dram of Glenfarclas, I was now in fine fettle.

There was a brief interruption to my idyllic environs when I was required to cross a road. I then headed down a lane, passing a sign for the 'Great Glen Water Park'. As far as I was concerned, the endless rain had made the entire Great Glen a water park and not a very fun one either... at least not like the water parks in Spain.

After a short stretch on an old railway line, I passed through a gate and took to a narrow path along the eastern shore of Loch Oich. I liked the sound of Loch Oich. It sounded like someone trying to grab your attention just

Walk This Way

as something catches in their throat. If ever a loch needed an exclamation mark, it was Loch Oich! Not that it was remotely grand in scale. This skinny body of water was only four miles long and as well as being the smallest of the three lochs linked by the Caledonian Canal, it was by far the shallowest. In fact, during the canal's construction Loch Oich had to be partly dredged so as to make its waters navigable. The Caledonian Canal reaches its highest point at Loch Oich at just over one hundred feet above sea level.

When I reached a particularly nice spot by the loch shore, I decided to treat myself to a quick break and a mid-afternoon snack. I delved into my bag and pulled out the prize of a Tunnock's Teacake. It had been on the tray – next to the complimentary tea and coffee – in my room at the B&B in Spean Bridge. I had resisted scoffing it at the time, preferring to save it for the road... and now that moment had arrived!

My Tunnock's Teacake Party at Loch Oich was a roaring success. And as I munched on that irresistible combination of chocolate, marshmallow and crumbly biscuit base, two canoeists paddled by. I gave them a wave. I'd have thrown them a couple of Tunnock's Teacakes if I'd had any spare.

Party over, and on the move again, I was soon back on the old railway line, which ran above the shore and trailed into the distance. I drifted off into another one of my daydreams but was jolted out of it by the ringing of a bicycle bell, right in my ear, as two cyclists overtook me.

I'd only just recovered from that surprise and fallen back into a trance when I got the fright of my life, with a loud 'hiya!' in my lug as a solo biker whizzed past. I jumped a mile and would have much preferred it if he had rung his bell instead. There was certainly more activity on this stretch of the Great Glen Way and the next person

I encountered was a young woman marching south. She had walking poles and a large backpack and I responded to her smile with a confused look. I could have sworn I'd passed the same woman yesterday. Was she repeating parts of the Great Glen Way or did she perhaps have a twin sister lagging a day behind her? It did not compute...

More troubling were the increasingly frequent signs along the disused railway line warning of the potential for falling boulders. While the loch lay to my left, a hill rose abruptly on my right and it was littered with boulders. I stared at them for any signs of movement and wondered if I would have sufficient time to jump out of the way if one of them did start hurtling towards me. Increasing my level of concern were the giant boulders lying to the left of the path, close to the loch shore. Giant boulders that had presumably tumbled down the hill at some point. One of them (the size of an asteroid, basically) was covered in moss and might have landed hundreds of years ago. Perhaps one of similar size was due to crash across the path today. I looked at the boulder-strewn hill again and sped up.

At least there was no danger of me being smashed to smithereens as I made my way through a spooky tunnel that seemed more suited to an episode of Scooby-Doo. Re-emerging into the light, I then left the old railway line and returned to the towpath of the Caledonian Canal, with Loch Oich now behind me.

It was a particularly lovely stretch of the canal as I walked the final few miles to Fort Augustus but the beauty was not matched by the weather since it was chucking it down again. After a couple of grim miles of trudging forth in the torrential rain, I reached Kytra Lock with its lock-keepers cottage. The Caledonian Canal then broadened as I closed in on my day's destination.

At the back of six, I stumbled into the village of Fort Augustus, which lies on either side of a flight of five locks. I made straight for the pier to clap eyes on Loch Ness whose waters were so grey and choppy, it looked more like a sea. I stood on the edge of the pier, being battered by the wind and rain but nothing could wipe the grin off my face. Loch Ness sounded a long way from Glasgow and indeed it was. I found it hard to believe that I had walked this far in the space of a week. But it was time to beat a retreat and find some much-needed shelter. I'd be seeing plenty of Loch Ness in the coming days as I zeroed in on Inverness.

I ducked into the nearest pub and stood at the busy bar, waiting my turn to be served. An English tourist was in the process of ordering dinner for his family.

'Two fish and chips and two kids' chicken meals... what do the kids' meals come with?'

'Chips,' replied the barmaid.

Her manner seemed abrupt but then I saw her swiftly deal with a couple of other customers at the crowded bar. She was keeping the chat to a bare minimum and everyone was being served quickly. Everyone was happy.

So, when it came to my turn, I simply stated: 'Pint of lager, please.'

'Three pounds,' said the barmaid.

I handed over the exact amount and my beer was promptly poured and served to me.

'Thanks,' I said.

I then went and sat down, letting the world's most efficient barmaid get on with the business of briskly serving the next wave of thirsty and hungry punters.

Once I'd finished my pint, I headed over to the hostel I was staying at. The place was filled with travellers from all over the world. There were Americans, Australians, Chinese,

Italians... but the first person I got chatting to was Thomas, who had a French-sounding accent.

'Are you from Belgium?' I asked.

'Yes!' said Thomas. 'How did you know?'

'Just a guess.'

— *Day Eight*
Great Glen Way
Fort Augustus to Drumnadrochit
Twenty-two miles

There were some interesting scenes at breakfast in the hostel dining room. A Japanese dude sitting down with a plate of baked beans and raisins... and another chap, possibly German, scrambling to prevent his boiled egg from rolling off the table (he wasn't quick enough).

I took a seat opposite a young Asian woman and wished her a good morning. She placed a hand over her mouth and started giggling. I cracked open my boiled egg and she chuckled some more. When I started spreading peanut butter on my toast, she dissolved into hysterics. I was basically the breakfast clown, purely there for her entertainment. I tried to consume my food in a manner that wasn't remotely amusing but failed miserably. I ate and she laughed. It was quite off-putting. Plus, the funniest person in the room wasn't even me. It was either that guy eating beans and raisins, or the other bloke chasing his boiled egg across the table.

Once I'd finished my unintentionally comical breakfast, I turned my attention to more serious matters. Such as walking another twenty-two miles in order to reach Drumnadrochit by nightfall.

I left Fort Augustus shortly after eight on a riverside path and then climbed a slope covered in pines before descending on a forest track, with good views of Loch Ness and a tiny island near the shore. Cherry Island – the only island on Loch Ness – was actually a crannog, an artificial island built centuries ago as a place of refuge.

When I came to a junction on the Great Glen Way, I had to choose between the high route and the low route. The former would take me above the trees for the next few miles, while the latter option stuck closer to the loch shore. I had no hesitation in going with the low route. My legs hadn't properly woken up yet and besides, I already knew from my map that I would have another opportunity to go high above Loch Ness a little later on, shortly after the village of Invermoriston.

In the meantime, the low track I'd settled for took me through a pine forest, with the trees largely obscuring the loch from view. I wasn't too bothered because in a couple of hours' time I would be gazing down on Loch Ness from a high vantage point. And while I was currently losing out on the epic loch views, I was enjoying the particular solitude and comfort of a cool forest walk, which I had grown to appreciate of late.

Also, the occasional gaps in the trees allowed me surprise glimpses of Loch Ness and I would stop, not wishing to take my eyes off the water for fear of missing out on something big. In other words, a rare sighting of Nessie. I was behaving just like I did when I was a kid and my parents took me on a Loch Ness boat cruise.

The fact is that Loch Ness is the deepest loch in Scotland and is also twenty-three miles long, so there is ample room for an ancient monster to dwell undisturbed. A friend of mine's grandfather claimed to have witnessed the Loch Ness monster many years ago. He was sitting in a pub close to the loch when he happened to look out of the window and saw a 'giant slug' cross the road. The giant slug helped itself to a sheep in a field before slithering back across the road and into the loch.

My friend's grandfather's description of the Loch Ness monster is so far removed from the more common 'sightings' of a humped serpent in the water that I'm inclined to believe him. Even if he had been drinking.

As I wandered among the oak and birch trees, I crossed a bridge over a burn and another one in front of a small waterfall. Eventually the track climbed around the shoulder of Sron na Muic and swung left into Glen Moriston. Following the path downhill, I soon reached the tiny village of Invermoriston where the River Moriston spilled beneath an old stone bridge. A sign outside the village hall read: 'Ceilidh Saturday at 8pm'. Ach, I was going to miss it. I was four days early.

But I did pop into the village shop where I picked up a classic takeaway lunch of tuna roll and packet of cheese-and-onion crisps. It was only after I had completed the transaction that I spotted the Tunnock's Caramel Wafers on the biscuit shelf. I couldn't resist making an additional purchase.

With lunch in the bag – or more accurately backpack – I ventured across the road to a rather posh-looking hotel. I quite fancied a cup of coffee and hoped that, despite the state of me, I might be served one. The receptionist was very welcoming and directed me towards a lounge where I promptly plonked myself down on a fancy sofa. I checked the carpet and was relieved to see that I hadn't left a long trail of muddy footprints.

'Would you like a scone with your coffee?' asked the

receptionist. I was fairly tempted but had just bought a packet of Caramel Wafers and would be tucking into them shortly while I walked.

'No thanks,' I replied. 'Just the coffee's fine.'

'Pancake?' she then suggested.

Hmm. Again, I was tempted but turned down the offer.

'Carrot cake?'

She really was pushing the suggestions of a sweet accompaniment to my coffee but once more I politely declined.

'Tunnock's Teacake?'

Now I did love a Tunnock's Teacake but I'd devoured one yesterday at my Tunnock's Teacake Party at Loch Oich. And the Caramel Wafers in my bag were made by the same confectioner. So, again, I said no.

But then she asked: 'Empire biscuit?'

The word 'Yes!' leapt out of my mouth.

Not in order to put a stop to her persistent line of questioning. It was just... who in their right mind would turn down an Empire biscuit? Not me. And now I was about to savour one, along with my coffee, in this plush lounge. Oh, what a life I was leading!

I got wired into my strong black coffee and managed to demolish the Empire biscuit without leaving any crumbs on the sofa. Now buzzing due to the amount of caffeine and sugar in my system, I rose to thank the receptionist for the incredible Empire Biscuit Experience (it didn't quite top the Tunnock's Teacake Party) and was on my way.

I then did a double take as I passed a clog shop. It was the last thing I expected to see in a small village in the Highlands – and the last thing I needed right now on my big walk was a pair of clogs.

Clogless, I left Invermoriston on a country lane that

zigzagged steeply up a hill and brought me to the edge of more forest and another choice of routes. This time, I favoured the high road over the low road. Having gone low in the morning, I was ready to hit the heights in the afternoon. I sought more drama plus my energy levels had rocketed as a result of that coffee and Empire biscuit combo. I faced a sharp initial ascent through the woods but it was nothing that my West Highland Way tested legs couldn't handle. After a sustained climb, I found myself clear of the trees, next to open moorland. I witnessed a bird of prey taking off from a rock but, being no expert, I wasn't certain what type of bird of prey it was. It definitely wasn't an eagle since it looked nothing like Sam from The Muppets.

Continuing along the high route, I then encountered a strange sculpture that consisted of tree branches woven into a circle. It was a bit too Blair Witch for my liking and I hurried past it. The track then turned away from the edges of the moorland and wound back into the woods.

I was feeling a little on edge and making matters worse was the mist that was rapidly closing in on me. So much so that when I reached a gap in the trees and tried to look down on Loch Ness, I couldn't see a bloody thing. The non-view of Loch Ness was a real kick in the teeth after all my hard legwork on the high route.

Trying not to be too frustrated and maintain some calm, I crossed a footbridge over a stream and wandered on among the trees until I spotted something on the path in front of me that brought me to a screaming halt. It was an arrangement of pine cones. They had been laid out across the path to form a single-word message.

HELLO

Instead of smiling at the greeting on the forest floor, I shuddered. Someone had clearly gone to a lot of effort with this pine-cone communication, but who? And why? Were they even watching me right now from behind a tree?

It was at this point that panic set in as I sidestepped the pine cones and took off down the path, while occasionally looking over my shoulder. That message could have said I'M WATCHING YOU or RUN but HELLO seemed just as bad. Was it the capital letters that made it menacing? Or the use of pine cones? I still had the image of that Blair Witch sculpture fixed in my mind too.

I felt fearful and far from anywhere… and it didn't exactly help when I then ran into 'Troll Bridge'. This curious, hand-crafted wooden bridge straddled a stream and looked like a prop from the movie Labyrinth. Next to 'Troll Bridge' was a display of colourful drawings of trolls, done by local schoolchildren. Most of the pictures were cute but a couple of them were quite terrifying. One even included a poem:

But wait there's the troll
I'm no longer on a stroll
I see his spear
I run with fear
I take a break
As he tries to hit me with a rake

Eh?

So, had the rake-brandishing troll laid out those pine cones on the path back there? Or were the schoolchildren responsible? If so, they were messing with my mind.

I ran across Troll Bridge then heard a rumble, only to realise that it was my belly. Lunch was long overdue but although I had a stash of food in my bag, I couldn't stomach stopping to eat any of it whilst stuck in this creepy forest far above Loch Ness. Instead I became more fatigued and rattled, my mind full of Blair Witch objects, demented pine-cone messages and trolls wielding pointy agricultural tools.

I staggered on and reached another gap in the trees but again there was no sign of Loch Ness below me. All I could see were the tops of distant mountains above the mist. Cue the onset of vertigo. This was like the Devil's Staircase but way worse. I had no Ailsa to dig me out of this awful situation. I didn't want to be up here on my own… I wanted down. What a mistake it had been to reject the low route. This was a disaster of my own making.

Trying to keep a lid on my growing panic, I spent a few moments talking to myself and trying not to focus on the scary mist-filled views. The only solution was to use my legs (current state: jelly) to get below the mist and off this hill as quickly as possible. But the only person who could achieve this was my terrified self.

I scrambled along the narrowing path, worried that I might trip and fall through the mist into the loch below. The creepy silhouettes of twisted trees that looked straight out of a Brothers Grimm fairy tale weren't helping my anxiety levels either. My only crumb of comfort was that the track now appeared to be descending. Down and down I went through the mist, the forest around me gradually becoming clearer.

After what felt like forever, I reached the junction with the low route where I bumped into two walkers. I'd never been so glad to see anyone in my life. One of the women held out a bag of nuts and offered me some. I gratefully accepted and took a handful.

'How are you getting on?' she asked.

'Um, well...' I said and proceeded to give them a breathless account of what I had just been through on the high route. I described the Blair Witch sculpture and 'Troll Bridge' and when I mentioned the pine cones, the pair of them burst out laughing, both agreeing it was creepy.

'How were the views?' I was asked.

'Couldn't see a thing,' I replied. 'I was surrounded by thick mist.' I was offered more nuts out of sympathy.

The bearer of the nuts was Anne, who was Scottish, while her friend Rachel was American. Doing the Great Glen Way together, they had just spent the morning enjoying the low route from Invermoriston. Yesterday they had walked the high route from Fort Augustus and had been knocked out by the incredible views of Loch Ness.

I'd done the exact opposite – going low then high – and had completely missed out on any kind of view but, hey, at least I got to terrify myself. Feeling spooked, giddy and completely cut off from the world had been an intense experience, if nothing else. You win some, you lose some... and I had almost lost my mind up there.

Setting the Loch Ness experience to one side, we compared notes on other sections of the Great Glen Way so far. I described battling through the rain to Laggan Locks and ducking into The Eagle for some much-needed shelter and refreshments (I didn't mention the wrong trousers incident). Anne and Rachel had sat outside the barge the day before in brilliant sunshine. They certainly seemed to be having more luck than me.

However, it was time for me to crack on (after almost cracking up in the woods above Loch Ness). Anne mentioned that there was meant to be a pottery up ahead with a cafe that they were looking forward to stopping by. 'Apparently, they do amazing cakes,' she said. I thanked her for this useful piece of information. I would for sure be looking out for this palace of pottery and tasty home-baking. Saying cheerio to Anne and Rachel, I set off along the level track while munching on my tuna roll and gazing across Loch Ness. After a while, I crossed a bridge next to a waterfall and then wound my way through yet more woodland, scoffing my packet of cheese-and-onion crisps and the first of my Caramel Wafers.

I soon spotted a woman walking towards me. As she got nearer, I saw that she had a walking pole in one hand and a fag in the other. One making her journey easier and the other doing anything but. She was also wearing a West Highland Way T-shirt. I presumed she knew that she was on the Great Glen Way.

The next person I encountered was a man rocking the double-denim look and walking two massive dogs.

'How's it going, big boy?' he asked me.

Big boy?

'Um, fine,' I replied before speeding up to be on my own again.

I then saw a sign for the pottery and cafe. Upon entering the place, I was hit with the smell of clay and coffee. I took a seat among the colourful pots, plates and vases, and I was served one of the strongest coffees I'd ever had in my life, which I enjoyed with some delicious ginger cake. Bolstered by the cake and coffee, I set off on the final stretch to Drumnadrochit, walking along a country road amid heather moorland and passing the occasional farm. The super-strong coffee had definitely put an extra spring in my step but after a mile or two, I began to flag badly. The passing-place signs by the side of the road may as well have been passing-out-place signs.

Eventually the Great Glen Way left the road for a

dirt path and I made a steep descent through woods to Drumnadrochit. I followed the River Coiltie into the village and passed a hall where bagpipers were practising, with the sound of Scotland the Brave blaring out of an open window.

After checking into my hotel and freshening up, I ventured out on a mild spring evening to explore Drumnadrochit, which has not one but two museums devoted to the Loch Ness monster. The window of one gift shop displayed Nessie inflatables, Nessie stuffed toys, Nessie key rings and even Nessie air fresheners. Already I was Nessied out.

I decided that it was time for dinner. Touristy Drumnadrochit wasn't short of dining options and I picked a restaurant where I ordered fish and chips. A group of young Americans at the next table were being a bit more ambitious in committing to the restaurant's special whisky-themed menu. For thirty quid, you received a starter of haggis with a whisky, followed by a main course of steak in a whisky sauce and, to round things off, pudding served with a further dram. I noticed that they also had a fair amount of wine on their table. They were going to sleep well tonight.

As was I, with twenty-two-more miles in the bag and another nineteen to look forward to come the morning.

— *Day Nine*
  Great Glen Way
  Drumnadrochit to Inverness
  Nineteen miles

After a hearty Scottish breakfast and a ridiculous amount of orange juice, I left my Drumnadrochit hotel, loaded with vitamin C and sausages. Food was still on my mind, though, as I swung by a shop where I queued behind a French family buying postcards and picked up a couple of morning rolls to sustain me in the hours ahead (I also still had a few Caramel Wafers left in my bag).

My departure from Drumnadrochit was hardly peaceful. It involved me walking along a pavement next to the busy A82. I finally received some respite from the cars and lorries when I swapped the kerb for a track that climbed between fields towards woods, with the bonus of a view of Loch Ness and the ruins of Urquhart Castle.

However, I then took a dim view of a sign saying: 'Great Glen Way diversion'. Was this diversion going to lengthen my walk or shorten it? Nothing was revealed besides an arrow, which I followed in good faith. It seemed to work out okay in the end as before long I was back on the regular route.

I walked on a mossy path in a dense forest that, thankfully, lacked the fright factor of yesterday's woodland above Loch Ness. This path was strewn with pine cones but none of them had been arranged to spell out any sinister messages. Although the sound of giant trees creaking in the wind was a little bit unnerving.

After crossing a stream via stepping stones, I faced a steep climb but it was worth the effort as I reached a viewpoint that took in much of Loch Ness. I sat down on a rustic bench consisting of a log balanced on two rocks. Etched in the wood were the names of walkers who had gone before me and who had also paused at this superb vantage point. There was an international flavour to the names: Pierre, Jael, Kamila. Knut, too. No doubt one or two of them were Belgian.

On I marched through the woods, eventually swapping the trees for heathery moorland before a winding and rising track led me into Abriachan Forest. As well as being enchanted by this ancient woodland, I was now at the highest point of the Great Glen Way at just over twelve-hundred feet. After wandering along the forest track for a couple of miles, I crossed a road and went through a kissing gate.

Now striding along a gravel path, flanked by bushes and heather, I became slightly puzzled when I saw a wooden sign with 'Bovril?' painted on it in colourful letters. A few moments later, I encountered a second sign, this one posing the question: 'Hot cocoa?' There followed a succession of these signs, each making a different beverage suggestion.

'Ovaltine?'

'Real coffee?'

All these signs were indicating that I must be approaching some kind of cafe in the middle of nowhere. Although after a while, as I passed yet more of them – 'Herbal tea?' – I began to suspect that there was no cafe and that instead it was some clever art installation in the Highland wilderness. Such a cruel trick to play on the exhausted and thirsty wanderer. But then, just as I was losing all faith in the possible existence of an oasis offering hot refreshments in the back of beyond, I reached a sign, with an arrow, telling me to turn off the main path now if I wanted to pay a visit to this mysterious cafe.

I duly did so and found myself trudging through mud and among chickens towards a building. I became confused when I reached a sign that stated: 'No authorised persons beyond this point'. Surely, I was approaching the much-advertised cafe? Stepping beyond the sign, I then hesitated due to the sense that I was trespassing.

As I stood stock-still in the mud, wondering what to do next (and suspecting that I should probably turn around now and return to the business of completing the Great Glen Way), a woman emerged from the building and started marching towards me in her wellies. Oops, I was in trouble now…

'Aye, you'll be looking for something to drink, a refreshment?' she called to me in a strong northern accent.

'Um, yes, that'd be great,' I said, still unsure as to where I was exactly and also feeling guilty about overstepping the mark. 'Sorry about me just walking past your sign there. I wasn't sure where to go.'

'Ach, there was a dinger before the sign but I think the blasted pig broke it,' replied the woman.

I was still trying to process this sentence as she led me back through the mud – the chickens scattering – towards a wooden shack. On the way we passed a large pig, presumably the one that had destroyed her 'dinger' bell.

'What's the pig's name?' I asked.

'Pest!' said the woman.

I was invited to take a seat on the veranda of the wooden shack. I did so and almost immediately a hen turned up at my feet, while ducks quacked close by.

'I'm Sandra, by the way,' said the woman. 'What would you like to drink?'

'A black coffee please,' I replied.

'Coming right up,' said Sandra.

And off she marched back through the mud, while I chilled with the hens and ducks. A short time later, Sandra returned, carrying a tray with a cafetiere of coffee, a mug and a plate of biscuits.

'Thanks very much,' I said. 'It's nice here.'

I was rather digging the place now. It was quirky and relaxing. Even with my friend the hen clucking and pecking next to me.

Sandra, my welcoming host who ran this place as an eco-campsite and coffee stop, was originally from Orkney, which explained the accent. 'Whenever I go back, folk say I sound like an Invernessian,' she sighed.

'You sound Orcadian to me,' I said.

I told her that I received similar comments whenever I popped back to the Moray coast from Glasgow. People would sometimes say that I'd lost my hometown accent and sounded like a Glaswegian. Whereas to most Glaswegians, I just sounded like your average teuchter.

Sandra's strong coffee tasted fantastic and I said so.

'You'll be fleein doon the hill after that!' she laughed.

I said that I was enjoying doing the Great Glen Way, discovering the Highlands at walking pace.

'Next time you're on a bus or a train, you'll feel like you're going a hundred miles an hour,' said Sandra.

We chatted some more until she announced: 'I'd better get back to the hoose, I'm makkin a pan of lentil soup with gammon'. I now wished that I was staying for lunch.

I promised Sandra I'd spread the word about her unique outdoor cafe. 'Only to nice people like you,' she countered. 'I don't want any grumpy sorts!' I laughed at that.

'Enjoy the rest of your journey and stay safe,' she said. 'The next bit's the best bit of the Great Glen Way – but I'm biased!'

Regardless of any local bias, I soon discovered that Sandra's statement held some truth as I made my way along a single-track road amid heathery moorland. To the northwest stood a formidable mountain whose summit was cloaked by clouds. I consulted my map and learned that it was Ben Wyvis.

I now had the bonus of a southerly wind behind me and this felt like the final push, at least as far as the Great Glen

Way was concerned. There was still the Speyside Way to come, but thinking about that just made me feel even more tired, so I put that to the back of my mind and focused solely on the present. I was going downhill now – at least in terms of terrain – and an elderly gentleman freewheeled past me on a bicycle. But I didn't mind. Pedal power was a wonderful thing, and cycling remained perhaps my favourite pastime, but I was genuinely content just to amble along on foot.

The next person to outstrip me was a runner, who smiled and said hello. A runner, a cyclist and a walker, all crossing paths in the Highland countryside... Normally I would be the cyclist, occasionally the runner but never the walker. I would have always put walking third in terms of preference and by some distance. But my views had shifted over the course of the past nine days. Cycling, running, walking, I liked them all. Each had their own challenges and benefits. It was all fresh air and exercise and all these activities offered that hard-to-beat feeling of achievement.

When the Great Glen Way left the country road for a dedicated path, I sat down and changed my socks, abiding by the rule that had served me well so far. Reinvigorated, I marched on and was soon strolling among ancient pinewoods where my feet were further soothed by the spongy, mossy path. The birds were chirping, the sun was shining and there was the sense that I was now on the final descent to Inverness with no more hills to climb. As a result of my growing anticipation, I broke into a jog. Then, through some birch trees, I caught a glimpse of sea. An uplifting sight and a sure sign that I was nearing the end of my Great Glen Way adventure.

I left the forest through a kissing gate and then passed a pond before the panorama opened up with an elevated view of the city of Inverness and the Moray Firth, as well as the Black Isle on the other side of the water. Following the track downhill between fields, I arrived on the outskirts of the Highland capital. I walked through an underpass complete with graffiti and a scrunched-up empty can of Special Brew. Then I skirted the edge of a golf course before being reunited with the Caledonian Canal one last time as I crossed a swing bridge.

I could now see Inverness Castle, the finishing point, as I strolled by a petanque club where men were throwing boules and shooting the breeze. Reaching the banks of the River Ness, I crossed a beautiful suspension footbridge to the lovely Ness Islands. A winding path, among the trees and daffodils, all too quickly led me to another footbridge, which I crossed to arrive on the opposite bank of the river. I then walked alongside the Ness and up the hill to the castle where a stone monument marked the end of the Great Glen Way. There were a few tourists milling around, so I dug out my phone and got one man to take a picture of me in front of the castle. I then headed across the road to the Castle Tavern for a celebratory pint.

I had completed the second leg of my cross-Scotland journey, walking seventy-five miles… no, seventy-nine, including that off-piste stroll to Spean Bridge… making it from west coast to east coast, from Fort William to Inverness, in four days. I'd walked the lengths of Loch Lochy, Loch Oich and Loch Ness – and spent many miles on the towpath of the Caledonian Canal, that astonishing feat of nineteenth-century engineering.

Yes, I had worn women's trousers and ran in fright from some pine cones. But I had also enjoyed a Tunnock's Teacake Party and drank Glenfarclas on a barge. Plus, I'd met Sandra from Orkney as well as various Zimbabweans,

Americans and (of course) Belgians.

While sipping my well-earned ale in the Castle Tavern's beer garden, I had a look at the picture the obliging tourist had taken of me. He had succeeded in fitting in all of the castle but had somehow managed to crop out my feet, surely the most important thing, the most relevant part of this story. When you want something done... do it yourself. But then that would have meant a selfie, which would be far worse than a wonky photo of me with my feet missing.

Ach, who needed a picture anyway? I had the memories... and the muscle pain.

SPEYSIDE
WAY

After catching an early train from Inverness I arrived in a cold Aviemore that hadn't properly woken up yet. There was little sign of life on the main street of the Highland resort town, save for the odd delivery van. I popped into a cafe close to the station for a warm-up coffee. I'd already had breakfast in the shape of a buttery, which I'd scoffed while half-asleep on the train. That buttery would probably keep me going until nightfall, such is the calorific quality of the Scottish croissant.

All caffeined up and heated up, I stepped back into the chill air and began walking down the street. I passed a few outdoor shops and a fenced-off piece of derelict land that was once Santa Claus Land, where every day was Christmas... This long-defunct tourist attraction – which featured Santa's grotto, a toy factory, sleigh rides and the actual North Pole – had been one of my favourite places as a kid growing up in the Eighties.

Despite dreaming about Santa Claus Land, I was alert enough to spot a waymarker for the Speyside Way, which led me out of town and onto a woodland path. While wandering among the trees, I was startled by a couple of early-morning joggers.

'Morning!' smiled the two women.

'Morning,' I mumbled back. In spite of that coffee, I was still rather sleepy.

The next person to greet me was a lady walking her dog.

'Morning!' she beamed. Everyone seemed so polite and

cheery in this neck of the woods. But then none of these perky locals had sixty-six miles of walking ahead of them.

The Speyside Way is a good deal shorter than the West Highland Way and isn't as long as the Great Glen Way either but coming straight on the back of those two, it was long enough. It was still going to take me three full days to hike from Cairngorms country to the Moray coast, following the course of the River Spey. Loch Lomond now felt like a lifetime ago, the Ledge of Doom but a distant memory along with those freaky feral goats. The Devil's Staircase now seemed less daunting looking back but the pine-cone message high above Loch Ness had retained its terror.

Leaving the woods, I encountered some shiny metal sculptures that were a bit War of the Worlds. Less alien were the Scots pines bordering a golf course. The Speyside Way then took me across heather moorland dotted with trees. The landscape was a pleasing palette of purple, brown and green, with a dab of white courtesy of the snow-capped Cairngorm mountains to the south.

It was raining off and on, the weather seemingly unable to make up its mind. There was the tiniest patch of blue overhead in an otherwise clouded sky but I wasn't getting my hopes up. The day's forecast was for persistent heavy rain. At least the underfoot conditions were excellent. The path across the moor was also intended for cyclists and I was soon passed by a couple of guys on mountain bikes.

Alone again, I started humming a tune. I Do Like To Be Beside The Seaside, of all the songs, but with 'Speyside' replacing 'seaside' in my head. I Do Like To Be Beside The Speyside worked rhythmically but otherwise made very little sense. Whilst humming my flawed version of a holiday classic, I heard a loud whistling sound. Rather than it being a fellow walker or a cyclist joining in with my catchy tune, it was the whistle of the steam train on the nearby Strathspey railway line. I couldn't see the steam for the trees but there was no mistaking that familiar sound.

The welcome whistle of the steam train, however, was followed by the sound of screaming. The source of the screaming became clear as a family overtook me on bicycles – Dad leading the way, followed by daughter and behind them Mum, pedalling while pulling a bike trailer containing her toddler son, who was busy crying his eyes out. He was not enjoying this family outing one bit. The poor child's face had been splattered with mud from Mum's back wheel. She stopped to wipe away some of the dirt and tears, then got back on the saddle and set off again. Within seconds, her boy began bawling once more. Even when they were out of sight, I could still hear him. Poor soul. And I thought I was having a hard time on Scotland's Ways...

The rest of what proved to be a short traipse across the moor passed quietly. Then I strolled down a leafy street full of grand houses as I arrived in Boat of Garten. Reaching the main road of this pretty village, I saw, on the opposite pavement, a man shouting at a post box. Until the car parked in front of the post box drove away to reveal the dog being given a good talking to by its owner, who I had assumed was off his head.

I then heard the whistle of the steam train again but this time spotted the white plumes of smoke rising behind some trees next to a hotel. I raced over just in time to see the vintage locomotive set off from Boat of Garten station on the next stage of its journey. A few tourists had gathered on the platform to witness the spectacle, with the train's passengers waving back to them from their carriages.

Once the steam train had departed, I ducked into the hotel to escape the rain for a bit. I thought about having another coffee but ended up just plonking myself down on a comfy couch in the lounge for five minutes in order to give my feet a rest and gather my thoughts. Then I was up again and out the door.

Having arrived in Boat of Garten in a state of confusion (due to shouty post-box man), I left the village in a similarly bewildered condition. Crossing the bridge over the River Spey was straightforward enough – and an early highlight of my Speyside Way journey since this was my first encounter with the iconic Scottish river – but then matters went slightly awry.

I found myself staggering along a grass verge by the side of the road, trying to avoid getting soaked by cars splashing through puddles, while hoping that I might stumble across an actual path. To my relief, I eventually found one fenced off from the road. The path led me to the entrance to Abernethy Forest where a sign informed me that within this National Nature Reserve I might expect to see red squirrels, pine martens and ospreys. It was a sure bet that I wouldn't see any of these fine creatures, given my atrocious track record with regards to spotting wildlife.

I did, though, hear a pleasing variety of bird calls, including one in particular which was really quite bizarre. I then realised that it was the distant whistle of the steam train on its way back to Aviemore. Still, it was a delightful stroll through these ancient Caledonian pinewoods – the rain had also ceased – and I especially enjoyed the option of being able to tread along a boardwalk to a lochan filled with reeds. It was such an atmospheric spot. In fact, the only thing missing from this idyllic scene was the presence of any woodland creatures... but then that was par for the course.

At one point during my forest wanderings, I passed through a beautiful glade where an elderly couple were sitting down, sharing a flask of tea and some sandwiches.

'Nice spot,' I commented.

'It is, isn't it?' smiled the woman.

I wanted to sit down, too, in this heavenly clearing but didn't wish to gatecrash their tranquil picnic. So I left the two of them in peace and continued on my way.

It wasn't long before I reached Nethy Bridge, 'The Forest Village' according to a sign. I popped into the village shop and picked up a sandwich and some crisps. I then sat down by the banks of the River Nethy, next to an old arched bridge, and scoffed my lunch before taking off my shoes and socks and cooling my feet in the river. I made sure they were totally dry before pulling on my two pairs of replacement socks. Ten days since setting off on my epic walking adventure, this ingenious sock system was still working a treat.

After crossing the bridge, I took to another disused railway line as I passed the old Nethy Bridge station, now a bunkhouse. Leaving the platform, I chugged along the grassy path towards Grantown-on-Spey and heard the whistle of the steam train again. At least it wasn't on this line, which hadn't been operational since the 1960s when it was closed under the Beeching cuts.

The walking was easy and pleasant, with the rolling countryside looking rather familiar to one raised amid the farmlands of Moray. Wandering past the ruins of Castle Roy, I then noticed a hill in the distance that looked like it had gone up in smoke. The source of the smoke was revealed when my old friend the steam train emerged from behind the hill.

While I was enjoying the gentle scenery and the regular sightings of the steam train, I wasn't having much fun with the horribly inconsistent weather. The returning rain and a strengthening wind soon turned what had been an agreeable amble across Speyside into something more arduous. I was beginning to feel drained of energy, though this no doubt had as much to do with the amount of miles I'd covered in the past week-and-a-half as the weather conditions. In need of a quick boost, I had a rummage in my bag and found a packet of shortbread fingers that I must have picked up from one of the hotel rooms during my travels.

I stayed on the straight and narrow of the old railway line, the shortbread fingers offering some crumbs of comfort in the harsh elements, while a flock of sheep in a field stared at me as if they were trying to figure out what on earth I was up to.

The Speyside Way was drawing close to the River Spey again and I noted that the water was moving at a fair rate. Quicker than me at least. The Spey is the fastest-flowing river in Scotland and is also the third-longest river in the country after the Tay and the Clyde. It is renowned for its world-class salmon fishing but I didn't have a rod handy. Neither did I have a fishing permit.

More than half of Scotland's whisky distilleries can be found in Speyside and I was hoping to sample a local dram or two en route, especially tomorrow when I was due to hit the heart of Malt Whisky Country around Aberlour and Craigellachie.

After crossing the splendid Spey via an old stone bridge, I walked along a quiet lane that led me to the edge of woods. Following a short stroll among the trees, I arrived in Grantown-on-Spey and wandered up the wide main street of this popular tourist town until I saw a pub that took my fancy and popped in.

I opted for a pint of locally brewed Wildcat and sat down at the bar. I got chatting to the barman and mentioned how I'd once spotted a wildcat near Perth. I then corrected myself and said that it was really more of a panther.

The barman smiled and nodded. There then followed a rather awkward silence. I was about to fill it by describing my panther sighting in more detail, when another punter approached the bar. This allowed the barman to go and serve their needs instead of having to stand about listening to the implausible chat of a worn-out stranger who had just claimed to have witnessed a panther in rural Scotland.

I picked up my pint of Wildcat and took a self-conscious sip, while feeling unfairly misunderstood. I did see a panther... I did!

— *Day Eleven*
  Speyside Way
  Grantown-on-Spey to Craigellachie
  Twenty-six miles

This was going to be epic and quite possibly painful. Twenty-six miles... TWENTY-SIX MILES... I had to stop fixating on the fact that I was about to walk twenty-six miles and that they would be far from flat, judging by my map.

Yep, the penultimate day of my tramp across Scotland was going to be a biggie. I was up against it – and dead against it too. But I had decided at the planning stage of this muckle adventure that Grantown-on-Spey to Craigellachie was within my capabilities.

Up bright and early, my eleventh day of walking began in a leisurely manner with a stroll across a golf course followed by a nice ramble through Anagach Woods. I admired the Scots pines whilst paying sufficient attention to the Speyside Way signposts, one of which had a woolly hat hanging on it. Someone somewhere was missing their cosy headwear.

Once through the woods, I sauntered along a path next to a pasture then reached the banks of the River Spey. I crossed an iron girder bridge and passed an old kirk as I approached Cromdale. Rather than walk through the village, the Way required me to leave the road and follow a path next to a field, then duck beneath a stone bridge to re-join the old Speyside railway line.

Yet, as I approached the bridge, something did not seem quite right. Near the archway was a fence post, on top of which was a shoe. As I drew nearer, I saw that the shoe – a trainer, in fact – was on the end of a leg. A seemingly detached leg, improbably balanced horizontally on the fence post. What was this grisly business? I hadn't the stomach for a crime scene right now. Or any time, come to think of it.

Horror turned to relief when all was revealed and it became apparent that the leg on the fence post belonged to a jogger, a mostly hidden jogger who was standing beneath the bridge doing some serious stretching exercises. 'Making an early start are you?' he asked, bringing his outstretched leg down from the fence post and planting it on the ground next to his other leg.

'Yep, I've not got much choice really,' I replied. 'I'm walking to Craigellachie.'

'Ooh that's a distance,' said the sprightly man, who looked to be in his sixties. 'You've got a tough morning ahead of you. Big climb through Tom an Uird Wood but once you get to Ballindalloch, it gets easier. It's just the first ten miles that are difficult. Best of luck with it all!' And with that, he jogged off in the direction of the River Spey.

Needing also to show some haste, given the number

of miles ahead of me, I set off along the old railway line, passing the former Cromdale station. Whereas the station building back at Nethy Bridge had become a bunkhouse, this one was now a private cottage. Standing next to it on the platform was a vintage train carriage that had been converted into self-catering accommodation. Though the curtains were closed, I could see the silhouettes of two children jumping up and down inside the carriage. No chance of a lie-in for Mum and Dad then.

A sign on a gate at the other end of the cottage read 'Lunatic Dogs' but I didn't investigate any further. There was also an old sign from the railway days, warning that trespassers on the line would be 'liable to a PENALTY not exceeding FORTY SHILLINGS'. I didn't have forty shillings on me. If caught, I could always ask if they took contactless. I marched eastwards, enjoying the feeling of the soft grass beneath my feet and the sight of fields turned golden by the morning sunshine. This was topped off by the uplifting sound of birdsong.

However, my smooth progress was soon interrupted by a succession of metal chain gates. In order to negotiate them, I had to unclasp them at the top, prise them apart and squeeze through the gap without them springing back into place and catching my trailing leg. These unexpected hinged contraptions were both awkward and time-consuming. They were making me unhinged.

After a mile or so of disrupted walking, I left the old railway line – and those wretched chain gates – behind as the Speyside Way bumped into the A95. I trudged along a grass verge for a hundred yards or so before carefully crossing the road and taking to a track through Tom an Uird Wood. This was the challenging section that the jogger back in Cromdale had forewarned me about and I was immediately hit with a steep climb among conifer trees, my first ascent of any kind since Loch Ness.

It was a shock to the system but after the track eventually levelled off I got more of a fright when I stumbled across a skeleton on the path. I couldn't quite tell what it was. My guess was that it was either a dog or a sheep (it definitely wasn't a brontosaurus). Although if it was a sheep, the nearest field was bloody miles away. A sheep couldn't have strayed this far... unless it had been dragged up through the woods. But what creature would be capable of doing that? Suddenly I was back on panther watch, peering through the trees and hoping not to catch sight of a jet-black beast in search of its next meal.

It didn't exactly help matters when, having stepped past the skeleton, I spotted a series of paw prints on the muddy path. They were large paw prints too. Possibly the paws of a dog but it would have to be a pretty damn big one... It occurred to me that the skeleton might be that of a deer rather than a sheep. But it could still have been a deer stripped clean by a panther.

This wasn't where I wanted to be right now, high and deep in these woods, all alone and fretting about the likelihood of there being a panther on the prowl. If only I had a walking companion to shake me and tell me that I was being ridiculous. But no, there was just tired old me, half-believing that my wholly irrational fear might be based on fact. As the self-styled hero of this epic journey, I didn't want to suddenly become its victim. The only thing I could think to do was scarper. And so I did, taking off through the trees like an idiot who imagined that they were at grave risk of being devoured by a big cat in the wilds of Speyside.

Another substantial forest climb slowed my progress but I kept on running while panting heavily like a doomed movie character seconds before they perished. On I sprinted, the track finally descending, quite steeply in places, until I collided with a gate and at last exited the forest to my considerable relief. I figured that my chances of survival had increased greatly now that I was out of the woods.

Then I remembered that the panther I'd witnessed all those years ago outside Perth had been lying in a field. And now that I had reached open countryside, I was surrounded by fields. Some of them were full of cattle but what if one of the many black cows was really a panther in disguise?

Stumbling downhill on a stony path, still on high alert with regard to rogue big cats, I then crossed a road to continue on a track between fields, with more of those flipping chain gates to contend with. I was making sufficient noise stomping about and battling with these awkward barriers that I scared a couple of pheasants and sent them scurrying across the countryside.

After crossing a wooden footbridge over a stream, I climbed to the top of a grassy scarp for a fine view across Speyside. I then ended up on a narrow path with bushes to my left and a low fence on my right. Just beyond the fence lay a big black cow, staring at. It wasn't a bull at least. But then it rose to its feet. It wasn't going to charge at me, was it? I so wished the fence between us was just that little bit higher... and that I wasn't so pathetic.

Clear of the cow, I fought through another series of chain gates before the Speyside Way rose steeply and skirted woodland. I then ended up on an extremely muddy track with barbed-wire fences either side of me. This was when I had my Looney Tunes moment. I was like the hapless Wile E. Coyote. It was so cartoonish. Even without the Road Runner going 'meep meep'.

The barbed-wire fences were keeping me apart from the

cattle but could not protect me from myself. When the muddy path deteriorated to the point where I resorted to jumping to reach the next available stone – just as I'd done on the West Highland Way – I suffered a comically painful sequence of events.

While negotiating the mucky obstacle course and readying myself for the next rock leap, I reached out to put my hand on the fence for support, quite forgetting that it was of the barbed-wire variety. 'Aah!' I cried out in pain before banging my head off an overhanging tree branch I hadn't noticed. The only thing that could have made this absurd episode more cartoonish would have been the ACME anvil falling from the sky and landing on my head.

Still reeling from the double whammy of hand on barbed wire and head against tree branch, I passed through a swing gate and slammed it shut, startling a few calves plus another pheasant which burst from a bush, smacked off a fence post and scuttled off across the field in a dazed manner. We were all in the wars this morning...

My next battle was another forest climb, this time through the woods of Knockfrink, which made me think of Batfink, the cartoon crime-fighting bat whose metallic wings were like a shield of steel. In an attempt to take my mind off the pain of having to scale yet another hill, I tried to recall as many cartoon heroes as I could from my 1980s childhood. Captain Caveman... He-Man... Dogtanian... Bananaman... Top Cat... Danger Mouse... by the time I got to Hong Kong Phooey I had made real progress through the woods. But truly I was heartily sick of my surroundings, having reached my limit in terms of being hemmed in by trees. I'd had it up to here with forests. See one and you've seen them all.

Still climbing through the dark woods and fresh out of

cartoon heroes – no, wait, Secret Squirrel! – I looked up from the forest trail to see the same view for the umpteenth time. Trees. I then encountered a man striding in the opposite direction with his two sons.

'Hi, how's it going?' the dad asked.

'Oh alright,' I sighed.

His friendly inquiry did not deserve to be met with such a grumpy response. Before I could snap out of my sulk and sound any cheerier, they were past me. It was nice to be asked but I'd been caught at a bad moment, selfishly feeling sorry for myself. At least I was a bit more jovial towards the woman I then met when leaving the forest. She was standing at a swing gate, with four kids clambering on it. Impressively, she had them all doing the Speyside Way. They were tackling it in the other direction and their target for the day was Cromdale. I asked how they were getting on so far.

'Pretty good,' smiled the woman. 'We'd be doing even better if this lot didn't insist on stopping at every gate and climbing on it!'

'Hmm, there are about fifty more gates between here and Cromdale,' I replied.

'Thanks for that!' laughed the woman.

They went their way and I went mine and I was soon wrestling my way through more chain gates as I followed another fenced-off path between fields.

I then crossed a burn via a footbridge and staggered along a dirt track before switching to a grassy trail and entering a wood full of conifers. I sighed at having to face yet another forest and swore too as I was forced to deal with another steep climb. I had thought that the Speyside Way would involve lots of pleasant strolling along the banks of the River Spey but the reality was much different. It was all forests and fields. After a descent through the trees and a short spell on a path alongside the A95, I crossed the road and ended up on another fenced-off track between fields. It was after this stretch that I was hit with a wholly unexpected and most unwelcome challenge.

Near a farm, the Speyside Way had degenerated into a major mud bath but making matters worse were the half-dozen cows lying in the mire. This time there was no fence between me and my bovine nemeses. The fact was that I was going to have to trudge amongst them for at least a hundred yards in order to reach the gate at the other end of the quagmire.

This wasn't what I'd signed up for! I wanted to do an about-turn but such a move was simply out of the question. I also wondered why that woman walking the Speyside Way with her children hadn't even mentioned this severe trial I was about to undertake.

I breathed deeply and took my first tentative steps, sinking into the mud up to my ankles. Swearing at my predicament, I squelched forward cautiously towards the cows. They were all ignoring me… apart from the biggest one, which stood up and faced me. Act calm, act calm, I muttered to myself. I even cracked a smile so as to appear friendly. 'He seems like a nice chap,' the cow may have been thinking. Or it might have been thinking: 'I'm going to trample him'. But then it might have been thinking… nothing. Whatever it was thinking whilst I was fretting, I made it safely past the cows and through the gate and onto a cattle-free path that wasn't a swamp. I had possibly just conquered my long-held fear of cows.

Just as I was feeling pretty good about myself, I almost stood on a frog. And then managed to frighten another pheasant, which went scurrying across a field. I was making a complete nuisance of myself in the countryside.

Trying not to upset any other creatures, I made my way down to the banks of the Spey. The river seemed to have sped up since yesterday. Whereas I, on the other hand, may have slowed down. I ground to a halt, sitting down next to the river and trying to cheer myself up with a spot of lunch. I demolished a cold sausage roll and scoffed an iced bun, both of which I'd picked up from a baker's in Grantown-on-Spey first thing before setting off.

Checking my map, it alarmed me that I'd only covered approximately half of the twenty-six miles required in this deranged stomp towards Craigellachie. Although to be fair to myself, the day so far had not been without its problems. In fact, I had been beset by difficulties from all directions.

Long forest climbs and cow-infested mud baths. That unidentified skeleton and the unsighted panther. Barbed wire and a badly situated tree branch, giving me sore hands and a sore head. A seemingly endless sequence of awkward chain gates. I'd had all that to put up with. What on earth would the afternoon hold?

I gulped down some water, changed my socks and got up. Then I followed the river downstream – though it was mainly hidden by trees – and was soon back on the old railway line where I bumped into two guys sharing their own Speyside Way adventure. Like everyone else it seemed, they were tackling it in the other direction from the Moray coast to Aviemore, which made me wonder if I was actually doing it the wrong way. Well, it was too late now. These two friends from Edinburgh were in the process of completing their own walking hat-trick. They had done the Great Glen Way last year and the West Highland Way the year before. They couldn't quite believe I was walking them all in one go.

'Seriously?' said one.

'Bloody hell,' said his pal.

They warned me about the section which they had just tackled and I was about to face. No mud baths, cows, skeletons, panthers or even hills. Just a lack of clarity regarding the actual path.

'Be careful,' said one of the guys. 'We lost half an hour going the wrong way.'

I ploughed on, paying full attention and not getting lost, and eventually reached the former Ballindalloch station, after which I crossed an old railway bridge above the River Spey. The Speyside Way continued to make use of the disused railway line, which curved according to the twists and turns of the river. After a couple of miles, I passed a distillery whose back door was ajar. My curiosity got the better of me as I stuck my head in and received an all-sensory experience: the impressive sight of the giant copper stills and the unmistakable whiff of whisky in the making. Well, I say all-sensory experience. I didn't get to taste the water of life. Although I would be doing just that in good time.

Removing myself from the door of the distillery, I returned to the business of walking the Speyside Way and it wasn't long before I passed another distillery at Knockando. Cousins of mine once lived there. In the village of Knockando and not the distillery, though their dad (and my uncle) could be considered Mr Whisky, having managed various Speyside distilleries over the course of his long career in the whisky industry.

Walking above the winding river, I heard the sound of a fishing rod being cast and looked down to see an angler at the water's edge, trying to catch some salmon or trout or perhaps a monster stickleback.

It was shortly after this that I hit a wall. And not a tiny wall either. It was about the height of the wall at Helm's Deep where King Theoden, Aragorn and Co were forced to defend themselves against the awful might of Saruman's Orc army. There remained parallels between my walk across Scotland and Frodo's epic slog across Middle Earth. I was charged with the quest of reaching Buckpool in one piece whereas the heroic hobbit needed to reach Mount Doom in order to destroy the One Ring. Sure, Frodo had the terrifying Ringwraiths and the devious Gollum to contend with but I had faced down multiple cows, coped with a traumatic episode involving pine cones and overcome the threat – real or imaginary – of a panther devouring me.

When Frodo was on his last legs in the depths of Mordor, he had his loyal friend Sam to carry him. Whereas I was utterly on my own. No one was going to give me a piggyback to Craigellachie. My ankles and knees hurt. My feet felt hot. I had pains in my shoulders while my lower back was sore too. The agonies were multiplying, plus I was almost out of water.

I sat down and changed my socks again and felt marginally better. According to my map, I had burst through the two-hundred-mile barrier. My head was also bursting. I stood up anyway and carried on, walking past the tiny village of Carron in a daze and crossing the Spey again. Still following the old railway line, I focused solely on the path ahead because anything else was beyond me by this point.

Eventually the town of Aberlour came into focus and my flagging spirits rose. I crossed a bridge over a burn and continued close to the river, passing a beautiful suspension bridge spanning the Spey. Aberlour is, of course, known for its malt whisky but it is also the home of Walkers shortbread.

I worked in the factory one summer as a teenager, baking shortbread fingers and shortbread petticoats in my white overalls and blue hairnet. After a tough, hot shift, I'd be absolutely stinking of shortbread. In fact, my brother was so upset by the stench that the second I returned home after my first day's work, he offered to spray me with the garden hose while I stood there fully clothed.

Now that I was back in Aberlour, it was more whisky I had on my mind than shortbread. Rather than swing by my former workplace, I dropped into the Mash Tun. This was no industrial accident in a distillery. The Mash Tun is the name of a pub and its whisky offering did not disappoint. There was a colossal amount of Glenfarclas on display in a large glass cabinet, with bottles dating back to the 1950s.

But as I was in Aberlour, I thought it would be rude not to go with the local whisky (even if Glenfarclas was only a few miles down the road). I went with the Aberlour Ten Year Old and the warmth of the whisky shot straight to my toes. I slumped back in my seat and savoured the rest of my dram – even though I knew that I'd have to get up again and march on. This was bliss but I still had two-and-a-half miles to go to Craigellachie. Would the whisky prove to be a help or a hindrance at this stage?

I mentioned to the barmaid that I was hoping to hit the Fiddichside Inn when I reached Craigellachie. She knew the landlord Joe. Everyone did. 'Joe's a fair age now,' she said. 'He keeps his own hours, opens when he likes.' I so hoped that he would be open. I'd been hearing about the legendary Fiddichside Inn for years but inexplicably – given that I hailed from Hopeman just twenty miles down the road – I had never set foot in this mythical boozer.

I hauled myself out of the Mash Tun and returned to the gravel path of the old railway line, enjoying the views of the Spey and saying hello to a woman walking her dog, a spaniel called Monty. It struck me that I was walking next to the Spey with a good measure of Speyside whisky in me. It felt good up top but I was not so sure that it was doing my legs much good.

I stopped to loosen the toggles on my walking shoes in an attempt to convince myself that I was wearing slippers and that this was all a breeze. But it didn't really work. A few hundred yards later, I was totally regretting that indulgent dram in the Mash Tun. I had treated Aberlour as the finish line. I should have abstained but, my goodness, it was great. I trudged through a long tunnel and finally reached Craigellachie, a tiny village which lies at the junction of two rivers, the Spey and the Fiddich.

Now for the Fiddichside Inn! I soon tracked it down, a whitewashed cottage idyllically situated next to the water. And it was everything I had imagined and wanted it to be. Picture the best pub in the world and double it. Walking into the Fiddichside Inn was like wandering into someone's living room. There was a fire on the go but instead of a sofa, chairs and a table there was just one long bar counter and a few stools. Behind the bar stood a smiling Joe Brandie, landlord of the Fiddichside Inn and in his late eighties. Joe had been serving drinks to customers for the best part of sixty years. He had run the bar together with his wife Dorothy until she passed away in 2009.

Joe, who had also been a cooper and a ghillie in his younger days, quietly asked me what I was after. I looked at his shelves of whisky bottles and asked for a Glenfarclas 105. As Joe went to pour my dram, I took in the instantly warming atmosphere of the Fiddichside Inn. There was no telly or jukebox, just a wee window with a view of the river, and conversations between customers.

There were all kinds of people here in this cosy wee room. Standing by the fire was a group of fishing types with posh English accents. One of the anglers chucked another log on the fire, stamped it down with his boot and nodded towards Joe behind the bar. 'I'll be in trouble if I don't do that!' he said to me, having kept the fire burning.

I received my whisky from the host and thanked him for it and said how brilliant I thought his pub was. 'It is quiet during the week but at the weekends it gets going,' smiled Joe. 'I can't complain.' He gazed out the window at the river below and then poured a pint for another customer (lager or export were your only choices).

I got chatting to a young German man in a kilt. Andreas was continuing his lengthy love affair with Scotland and had just driven the northern coastline.

'Ullapool... Durness... Wick... Brora,' he recited with impeccable Scottish pronunciation.

But this here was the highlight. Andreas simply adored the Fiddichside Inn. 'A special place,' he grinned, clinking his pint glass against my whisky glass.

The stools at the bar were mostly occupied by locals who lived dangerously close to this gem of a boozer. One man learned that I was walking the Speyside Way and bought me a drink. It turned out that his wife was from Hopeman and knew my mam. I met more people, had further conversations and was served more drinks by gentleman Joe. I didn't wish to be anywhere else in the world right now.

The Fiddichside Inn was the absolute pinnacle of pubs and though I had to get up in the morning and walk again, well, I'd somehow managed to put that to the back of my mind and was thinking about maybe having one more dram for the road.

It couldn't hurt, could it?

— Day Twelve
Speyside Way
Craigellachie to Buckpool
Twenty-three miles

Here it was then, the final day. One more big push from Craigellachie to the Moray Firth to conclude my springtime walk across Scotland and complete my hat-trick of long-distance walks. I crossed the bridge over the River Fiddich and winced at the sight of the Fiddichside Inn, scene of last night's over-indulgence. Truth be told, my head was a little cloudy, my hungover state matching the heavy sky. Why oh why had I got stuck into the cask-strength whisky in such a reckless fashion? Instead of feeling fresh for these momentous closing miles, I felt done-in.

A friend of mine had actually warned me about the dangers of the Fiddichside Inn while simultaneously singing its praises. He'd drunk there many a time and could never remember leaving. It was that kind of place.

Being barked at by a succession of dogs didn't exactly help my tender head as I passed a number of gardens. Once the canine chorus mercifully subsided, it was just me and the birds as I made my way along a quiet country lane lined with birch trees. There were a few chaffinches dotting about by the roadside. I recognised them from the bird wall chart in that Tyndrum cafe many moons ago. I wandered past a massive Speyside mansion and was then overtaken by a tractor that appeared to be attempting to break the world speed record for farm vehicles.

My last day's walking across the country was being conducted in cold and gloomy conditions but I didn't mind. I was Scottish enough not to care, plus it was probably better than trying to shake off a whisky hangover in bright sunshine.

After a couple of miles on the country road, the Speyside Way switched to a forest track as I embarked on a steady climb along the western slope of Ben Aigan. Now I was getting a workout. Although the sweat was as much a result of those ill-advised drams of Glenfarclas 105 as the actual exercise. The ascent did bring me fine views of the Spey Valley and I also caught a glimpse of the Moray Firth. The coast was clear and not too far away now. I began a long and gradual descent through the dense forest. My peaceful trudge down the jungle-like path was shattered by the noise of a chainsaw buzzing into action. Must be some forestry work underway nearby, I figured. Then I passed a sign warning of shooting in the area. Apparently this path skirted the grounds of the local gun club. Suddenly I was a bit jumpy, which I suppose was hardly unusual. Except that rather than me being put on edge by potential panthers, unpredictable cows or a weird arrangement of pine cones, it was the threat of stray bullets and an out-of-control chainsaw.

I'd calmed down by the time I joined a sandy track across farmland. I then bumped into the River Spey again and crossed an impressive iron bridge before continuing along a single-track road. Which was fine until I was caught out by a big hill, with the road rising steeply. And I'd thought I was done with climbing on this exhausting journey. Surely by now I should just be coasting it down to the mouth of the Spey, and the Moray Firth? But no.

I consulted my map. The offending hill was the Hill of Cairnty, which immediately leapt to the top of my list of most-hated hills. Even though this list was not as established as my list of most-loathed lochs. What upset me most about the Hill of Cairnty was that it was a sneaky hill in that it had crept up on me when I had least expected it. In its own way, the Hill of Cairnty was worse than the Devil's Staircase. I'd been able to build myself up for that one. Even though it had still reduced me to a gibbering wreck.

Despite the unwelcome uphill, it was a scenic journey along the high road to Fochabers, with splendid views across green countryside. The landscape around me had become more gentle and reassuring. This was Moray alright. I felt like I was home – the home of my childhood – having left my house in Glasgow close to a fortnight ago.

I heard a whooshing sound and wondered if there was a waterfall nearby then realised that it was the wind rushing through the trees. This was all rather pleasant. Until I received another nasty surprise. Having to tackle a canyon definitely wasn't in the script. It wasn't exactly the Grand Canyon but it was still of sufficient depth to almost break me.

The twisting road dropped sharply to the base of the surprise gorge and rose equally steeply on the other side. I braced myself for this down-and-up ordeal and began my descent. Immediately both of my kneecaps protested heavily. Then my thighs threatened to quit. This was agony, without doubt the worst pain of the journey so far. I had clearly just about reached my limit and this canyon caper wasn't helping me any.

I struggled to the bottom – half-thinking that I might pass out – then tried to gather myself for the ridiculous climb up the road to the top. Bizarrely, the ascent wasn't actually as bad as the descent. It was still exhausting and sore on my legs – an uphill that was almost steep enough to require crampons – but my knees seemed better able to cope with it. Scrambling out of the canyon, I came to a car park for the 'Earth Pillars' viewpoint. What on earth were Earth Pillars? Even though my legs felt like pillars, I decided to investigate. A short path led me through Scots pines to an elevated view of the River Spey and fields beyond. But the view was somewhat marred by the giant pylons spread across the landscape. It wasn't so much the Earth Pillars viewpoint as the Ugly Pylons viewpoint and I still didn't know what Earth Pillars were. Down below by the riverbank, two anglers seemed to be shouting at each other. From up here, I couldn't tell whether they were arguing or not. It was hard to imagine an argument breaking out during a spot of salmon fishing.

'My fish is bigger than your fish!'

'Is not!'

'Is!'

'Well, my rod is bigger than your rod!'

'Is it heck!'

'Is so!'

I forgot about the warring fishermen and scoffed a few oatcakes before changing my socks and setting off along the narrow road to Fochabers. I was soon passed by a jogger. 'Nice day for it,' he remarked. It wasn't a nice day in the slightest. It was cold and windy and it had just started to rain. He was being sarcastic.

I traipsed on in the deteriorating weather. A car came towards me and I stepped off the road, gripping on to a fence with one hand while giving the driver a wave. But she just stared straight on. What is it with people? Perhaps she had something on her mind.

Minutes later, I stepped onto the grass for another car, this one pulling a horsebox. The woman returned my wave and smiled too, which lifted my spirits.

As I entered the village of Fochabers, a joiner working on a house said: 'Aye, aye'. His manner of greeting confirmed (as if I didn't know it already) that I was firmly in Moray territory. Approaching the high street, I stepped off the pavement to overtake a mother pushing a pram, with her other child walking alongside her. Once past them, I heard the mother shout at her son, telling him to get off the road. 'He's on the road too!' the boy protested, meaning me. Realising that I was setting a bad example, I stepped back onto the pavement.

I walked past a fish and chip shop that had a giant banner proclaiming it to be one of the best fish and chip shops in the country. However, it wasn't open, so I settled for a sandwich and crisps from a shop. I then sat down in the village square next to the church and clock tower – the rain had temporarily ceased – and quickly scoffed my makeshift lunch. It had just gone one o'clock and I had ten more miles to go. Five to Spey Bay and another five along the coast to the finish line at Buckpool harbour.

I returned to the waymarked path and passed beneath a busy road bridge. Baxters stood on the opposite side of the river. My late father-in-law had a long and successful career with the famous Scottish food company. Whenever Dave visited me and my wife in Glasgow, he would bring down a car boot-load of Baxters produce. We were never short of cans of soup and jars of marmalade and beetroot in our house.

The Way left the river bank and wound through some woods as it occurred to me that I had yet to meet a fellow walker on my final day. Right now it was just me and a bumblebee. Then a dog bounded towards me, an excitable spaniel with a stick between its teeth. It dropped the stick at my feet. I barely had the strength to bend down and pick it up but did, throwing the stick further along the path for the dog to chase after it. 'You kept him happy,' smiled its owner, arriving on the scene.

I wasn't happy about my back right now, I wanted to tell the man. And my back wasn't happy with me for being roped into a spot of stick-related gymnastics. I plodded on – no longer wincing – as the track passed through swathes of yellow broom, the sight and the scent of it so tied to my Hopeman childhood, much of which was spent on the golf course. Then I reached a sign warning about giant hogweed. 'Caution. May cause irritation.' Even at this late stage there was the potential for me to do myself some damage. And there was time yet for that panther to leap out of the bushes and claw me to pieces.

The path then brought me close to the Spey again, the river now at its widest, just a mile or two from the sea. The Spey begins as a tiny burn high in the Monadhliath mountains, west of the Cairngorms, and here it was a hundred or so miles later, swirling and speeding towards the Moray Firth.

As I closed in on the coast, I finally met some other long-distance walkers, a mother and daughter marching with backpacks in the opposite direction.

'Speyside Way?' I asked.

'Yep, just getting started,' said the mother.

'I'm just finishing. All the best!'

'Thanks!' they both smiled.

Seagulls flapped overhead as I neared the sea and I thought I could hear the sound of waves on shingles. There used to be a salmon fishing station at the mouth of the Spey. The old ice house still stands. In fact, I could see it now but I was more interested in the small gathering of people in front of the ice house. I gave them a wave and they waved back. For this was my welcome party.

Four generations of my family: my granny, my mam, my

sister, my six-year-old daughter and four-year-old son. My wife and my mother-in-law too. Plus cousins. I had phoned Hopeman from Fochabers to give them an estimated time of arrival at Spey Bay.

'Well done, Gary!' smiled my mam, giving her eldest and exhausted son a hug.

'Cheers, Mam,' I replied. 'But I've still got five miles to go.'

My granny couldn't understand why the Speyside Way didn't just finish here at Spey Bay where the river meets the sea. I shared her viewpoint and explained to her that this used to be the end – or start – of the Speyside Way but in recent years it had been extended along the coast to Buckpool. 'They added a bit,' I sighed.

'They've no business doing that!' said my granny.

I liked how indignant she sounded, as if they had extended the Speyside Way simply to make her grandson's life more difficult. She was on my side.

Instead of all standing around chatting in the cold, we ducked into the cafe at the Scottish Dolphin Centre, which is next to the old ice house. The mouth of the Spey is a popular feeding ground for the bottlenose dolphins of the Moray Firth. I'd have liked to have witnessed a dolphin but didn't have time to stand around staring at the sea.

Coffees were ordered by the adults, the kids were treated to ice cream and I took my leave of my family because I still had a walking mission to complete. We agreed to meet up at Buckpool harbour and celebrate the true end of my trekking adventure.

'How long will you be, an hour?' asked my mam.

'Eh?' was my only response to that question.

It was five miles to Buckpool and the average walking speed was three miles per hour. My energy levels were so depleted by this point that I was surely doing worse than the average.

'More like two hours,' I suggested.

Everyone wished me good luck and I set off on the final stretch along the Moray coast to Buckpool. I passed a derelict hotel then entered some woods, the path winding through conifer trees next to a golf course. Nature called, so I left the path and nipped into the trees. When I ducked back out again, I gave a man out for a walk the fright of his life. He actually leapt off the ground. 'Made me jump for a minute there!' he exclaimed, trying to regain his composure. 'You came out of nowhere... I was in my own bubble.' Nothing wrong with being in your own bubble. But there is something wrong with jumping out from behind trees. I duly offered the shaken gentleman my apologies.

I carried on through the woods without frightening any more locals and eventually emerged from the trees to join another old railway line. I followed the grassy path for a stretch before ending up on a road which brought me to the seafront at Portgordon. I gazed out at the grey and choppy Moray Firth and then checked my map: two more miles to go. After walking along the long esplanade and leaving Portgordon behind, I found myself on a coastal footpath and spotted a group of seals lying on the rocks. A car then pulled up alongside me. It was my wife, with the kids in the back.

'Isabella wants to join you,' said my wife. I opened the back door of the car and my daughter got out.

'Ready for a wee walk?' I said to Isabella, taking hold of her hand.

'Okay, Daddy,' she beamed.

Clare drove off, with Alexander waving out the back window. And I walked the final mile of my cross-country journey in the company of my daughter, chatting to her and realising I was now walking on air. This was without doubt the perfect ending. We wandered along the pavement together, passing the 'Welcome to Buckie' sign. The old fishing village of Buckpool is essentially part of the bigger fishing town of Buckie nowadays.

Isabella and I reached the harbour where our family were waiting for us. All that remained of Buckpool harbour were the old harbour walls and a small playpark where the pier had been filled in some years ago. It seemed an odd end to the journey, not quite what I was expecting. But what did it matter? What was important were the miles and they were now complete. Job done.

'Well done, Daddy,' said my daughter, gazing up at me.

'Well done, Isabella,' I replied. 'You've just completed the Speyside Way!'

I lifted her up and gave her a big hug.

I then sat on the harbour wall and had my picture taken, giving the thumbs up with the Moray Firth behind me. Also behind me were two hundred-and-forty-one miles that had taken in Loch Lomond, Rannoch Moor, the Devil's Staircase, the foot of Ben Nevis, the Caledonian Canal, Loch Ness, the River Spey, the legendary Fiddichside Inn and much more besides.

It had been some journey, which I'd planned and accomplished.

Now it was time for me to put my feet up.

— *Day Thirteen (six months later)*
The Speyside Way
Buckpool to Buckie
Half-a-mile

Here we go again... I am back at Buckpool harbour. Back where I finished, except that turned out to be a false ending.

It was only some months after completing my walk across Scotland that I discovered to my dismay that I hadn't actually done all of the Speyside Way. I'd somehow missed a bit... the last bit.

As far as I was concerned, it wasn't my fault. The map I'd bought in good faith in a Glasgow bookshop – along with maps of the West Highland Way and Great Glen Way by the same publisher – had clearly charted a route between Aviemore and Buckpool harbour. I had also checked out various websites – including Wikipedia – during the course of my pre-trip research and all of them stated that the Speyside Way was a sixty-six-mile walk between Aviemore and Buckpool. So why would I think that the reality was any different? I would walk from Aviemore to Buckpool and conclude my mission. And then write up the whole experience.

It was during some post-trip fact-checking that I stumbled across a website which stated that the Speyside Way was a walk between Aviemore and Buckie. They surely meant Buckpool. But I did some further googling anyway and was gobsmacked. The Speyside Way originally ran between Aviemore and Spey Bay but in the late Nineties the route was extended to Buckpool harbour. I'd followed that to the letter. But seemingly at some point more recently – certainly before I'd walked the route – the Speyside Way had been expanded once more to Cluny Square in the centre of

Buckie, and Buckpool harbour was no longer the target.

I hadn't got the memo. Neither had the mapmaker, whilst the information on lots of websites was also out of date. Presumably at some point in the future the Speyside Way will be stretched beyond Buckie to, say, Peterhead, or even Bergen in Norway.

I'll be honest: I was hugely frustrated. I'd walked for twelve days across Scotland and thought I'd nailed my hat-trick of iconic walks but the unavoidable truth was that I had fallen agonisingly short. I couldn't simply leave it like this. It was like a full stop missing on the final sentence. I had been robbed of a full sense of accomplishment.

So here I go again. Back at Buckpool harbour where I finished. I suppose I had better get started then...

My son, almost five now, has joined me for the actual grand finale. Alexander is shivering. Not with excitement but because it's freezing. His little teeth are also chattering on this bitterly cold autumn day. There's a northerly wind sweeping in from the Moray Firth and hitting us in the face, plus it's just started raining to complete the miserable picture. I could have planned this better.

I hold my son's hand tightly and say: 'Are you okay?'

'Can we go now, Daddy?' he asks.

I'm not sure if he means start walking, or go home. I hope it's not the latter because we can't go home just yet. We have work to do. Unfinished business. The fulfilment of a mission which I thought I had achieved months ago, but never mind. It happened and we're here now, having just been dropped off by my wife and daughter who have headed to a warm cafe in Buckie's town centre to eat cake and await our arrival.

Alexander and I are both wrapped up at least. My son has on a thick coat and a Batman woolly hat and non-superhero woolly gloves. I'm wearing all my gear. The John-approved waterproof jacket, the waterproof trousers over my walking trousers, the tattered baseball cap, the indestructible boots and the two pricey pairs of socks. My backpack is pretty empty for this concluding half-mile hike, but still. I'm taking this seriously because it is a serious matter.

We depart Buckpool harbour and walk along the pavement next to the main road towards Buckie proper. The wind and rain are a pain but I'm enjoying the company. Even if my son is struggling to enjoy it. I offer to pick him up and carry him but he shakes his head. He's fine walking. These Sutherlands are built of strong stuff.

The two of us hardy northern souls – son and grandson of the late Captain James, whose boat the Adonis once sailed out of Buckie – turn away from the sea and start heading up the hill towards windswept Cluny Square. Our journey ends with us entering a small grass park and walking past some benches to reach two stone markers, signifying the start – or, in our case, the finish – of the Speyside Way.

I place a hand on one of the stones and get Alexander to do the same. We stand there for a moment in the wind and rain, smiling at each other, and I think my son has a sense of what this means. That his dad is daft, yes, but also that together we have achieved something. And even if he soon forgets about it, I will always remind him of our joint success.

My walking journey – finally – is complete. My son and I leave the end of the Speyside Way and head to the nearby cafe where Clare and Isabella are waiting. Alexander and I march into the cafe as intrepid adventurers.

'How did it go?' asks my wife.

'It was tough,' I sigh. 'But it's done.'

'Can I get you a coffee?' she asks.

'Go on then.'

'Can I have a cake?' asks Alexander, clocking the piece on his sister's plate.

'Of course,' I smile.

He has only just completed the Speyside Way at the age of four.

That boy will go far. Just like his dad did.

ACKNOWLEDGEMENTS

Thanks to Martin Greig and Neil White at BackPage Press, cover designer Chris Hannah, outdoor guru John, Alan Rowan, Charlie McGarry and to my family for their love and support. I also raise a glass to the late Joe Brandie.

Gary Sutherland
February 2018

ABOUT THE AUTHOR

Gary Sutherland is a writer from Hopeman in Scotland. He is the author of Walk This Way, Golf On the Rocks, Life Cycle, Hunting Grounds, Great Balls of Fire and Classroom Superheroes. He also danced with Prince and makes music as DJ ZX Spectrum. More at garysutherland.co

ALSO BY THE AUTHOR

Golf On the Rocks
Life Cycle
Hunting Grounds
Great Balls of Fire
Classroom Superheroes